Bank Statement Mortgage Loan Mastery

How to Qualify for a Mortgage Using Bank Statements Instead of Tax returns

By Joseph G. Correa

Licensed Mortgage Broker, Finibi Mortgage

Copyright & Legal Notice

Published by Live Stronger Faster

The information provided in this book is for educational and informational purposes only and does not constitute financial, legal, tax, or investment advice. Although the author is a licensed mortgage professional, the content presented is general in nature and is not intended as personalized guidance for any specific individual or financial situation.

The strategies, structuring methods, and examples discussed in this book are illustrative and educational in nature. They are intended to demonstrate concepts related to bank statement mortgage loan qualification and structuring, including deposit analysis, expense ratio application, and investor guideline interpretation. These examples do not represent guaranteed outcomes or approvals. Results may vary significantly based on individual financial profiles, documentation, credit history, property type, and lender-specific requirements.

The author and publisher make no representations or warranties regarding the accuracy, completeness, or applicability of the content and disclaim any liability for errors, omissions, or outcomes resulting from the use or misuse of the information contained in this book.

All trademarks, service marks, company names, and product names referenced in this publication are the property of their respective owners and are used strictly for identification and educational purposes only. Their inclusion does not imply endorsement or affiliation.

First Edition, 2026

Table of Contents

Introduction

In today's lending environment, the traditional path to qualifying for a mortgage does not work for everyone. For decades, banks and lenders have relied heavily on tax returns, W-2s, and standardized income documentation to determine whether a borrower qualifies for a home loan. While this system works well for salaried employees with predictable paychecks, it often fails to accurately represent the financial strength of millions of individuals who earn income in more flexible, entrepreneurial, or non-traditional ways. This includes self-employed professionals, independent contractors, freelancers, business owners, and 1099 earners—individuals who may generate substantial income but structure their finances in ways that minimize taxable income on paper.

This is where bank statement mortgage loans come in.

Bank statement mortgage loans are designed to solve one of the biggest challenges in modern lending: how to fairly and accurately assess income for borrowers who do not fit into traditional underwriting models. Instead of relying on tax returns, these programs allow borrowers to qualify based on their actual cash flow as reflected in their bank statements.

This approach offers a more realistic picture of a borrower's financial health, especially for those who write off expenses, reinvest into their businesses, or operate in industries where income can fluctuate month to month.

This book is the foundation of a powerful series designed to help you fully understand, qualify for, and strategically use bank statement mortgage loans to achieve your real estate goals. Whether you are trying to purchase your primary residence, invest in rental properties, refinance an existing loan, or access equity, mastering this loan type can open doors that traditional financing may have closed.

At its core, a bank statement mortgage loan evaluates income differently. Instead of asking, "What did you report to the IRS?" the lender asks, "What money is actually flowing through your accounts?" This shift in perspective is critical. It allows borrowers to leverage their real income rather than their taxable income, which is often reduced due to legitimate business deductions. For example, a business owner may earn $200,000 in gross revenue but show only $60,000 in taxable income after expenses. A traditional lender would base qualification on the $60,000 figure, while a bank statement lender may evaluate the full cash flow and determine a much higher qualifying income. Understanding how lenders analyze bank statements is one of the most important skills you can develop as a borrower or mortgage professional. Lenders typically review either 12 months or 24 months of bank statements to calculate average monthly income. These statements can be personal accounts, business accounts, or a combination of both, depending on the program and the borrower's profile. Each approach has its own advantages, and choosing the right one can significantly impact your approval odds and loan terms.

The difference between 12-month and 24-month programs is more than just the number of statements required. A 12-month program may allow you to qualify faster and with less documentation, but it may also show more volatility if your income fluctuates. A 24-month program, on the other hand, can smooth out inconsistencies and provide a more stable average income, which may lead to stronger approvals. Knowing when to use each option is a strategic decision that can make or break a deal.

Another key distinction in bank statement lending is the use of personal versus business bank statements. Personal bank statement programs typically analyze deposits into a borrower's personal account, often assuming a standard expense factor if the borrower is self-employed. Business bank statement programs, however, may require additional documentation such as a profit and loss statement or a letter from a CPA to determine how much of the business revenue can be used as qualifying income. Each method has its own underwriting guidelines, and understanding these differences allows you to position yourself in the strongest possible way.

Who qualifies for bank statement mortgage loans? The answer is broader than most people realize. These programs are specifically designed for individuals whose income cannot be easily documented through traditional means. This includes self-employed borrowers who own businesses, 1099 contractors who receive income without W-2s, gig economy workers, real estate investors, consultants, and professionals in industries such as sales, marketing, technology, and creative services. If your income is real but not easily captured on a tax return, there is a strong possibility that a bank statement mortgage loan could work for you.

However, qualification is not automatic. Lenders still evaluate key factors such as credit score, down payment, loan-to-value ratio, reserves, and overall financial profile. While bank statement loans are more flexible in terms of income documentation, they often require stronger compensating factors in other areas. For example, a borrower with a lower credit score may need a larger down payment or more reserves to offset the perceived risk. Understanding how these pieces fit together is essential for building a strong loan file. This book will guide you through all of these concepts step by step. You will learn what bank statement mortgage loans are, how they work, who they are designed for, and how to position yourself for approval. You will gain insight into how lenders calculate income from deposits, how expense factors are applied, and how to avoid common mistakes that can lead to denials or unfavorable terms. By the end of this book, you will have a clear understanding of the fundamentals that form the foundation of the entire series.

As you move through the Bank Statement Mortgage Loan Mastery Series, each subsequent book will build on this foundation. You will dive deeper into personal bank statement strategies, business bank statement analysis, advanced structuring techniques, refinancing options, and specialized scenarios such as jumbo loans and investment properties. The goal is not just to help you get approved for a loan, but to give you the knowledge and confidence to strategically use these programs to grow wealth, create opportunities, and take control of your financial future.

One of the most important mindset shifts you must make is understanding that lending is not just about meeting requirements—it is about structuring your profile in a way that aligns with lender guidelines. Two borrowers with identical income can receive completely different outcomes based on how their financial information is presented. This is why knowledge is power. When you understand how lenders think, you can position yourself to win.

Throughout this book, you will also begin to see patterns in how successful borrowers approach bank statement loans. They are intentional about how they manage their accounts, how they document their income, and how they prepare their loan files. They do not leave approval to chance. Instead, they build a strategy before they ever apply. This proactive approach is what separates those who struggle to get approved from those who consistently succeed.

In today's economy, flexibility is more important than ever. The workforce is evolving, and more people are choosing to work for themselves, build businesses, and create multiple streams of income. Traditional lending guidelines have not always kept pace with these changes, but bank statement mortgage loans represent a powerful alternative that aligns with the realities of modern income.

This book is your starting point.

Whether you are a borrower looking to buy your first home, an investor seeking to expand your portfolio, or a mortgage professional aiming to better serve your clients, the knowledge you gain here will provide a strong competitive advantage. You will begin to see opportunities where others see obstacles. You will understand how to navigate complex scenarios with confidence. And most importantly, you will learn how to turn your real income into real approvals.

Welcome to the Bank Statement Mortgage Loan Mastery Series.

Chapter 1

What Are Bank Statement Mortgage Loans and Why They Exist

Bank statement mortgage loans were created to solve a fundamental mismatch between how modern people earn income and how traditional lenders evaluate it. For decades, mortgage underwriting has relied on standardized documentation such as W-2s, pay stubs, and tax returns to determine a borrower's ability to repay a loan. While this system works efficiently for salaried employees with predictable earnings, it often fails to accurately capture the financial reality of self-employed individuals, business owners, and independent contractors. As the workforce has evolved, with more people earning income through flexible, entrepreneurial, and non-traditional means, the need for alternative documentation programs has grown significantly. Bank statement mortgage loans are one of the most powerful solutions to emerge from this shift.

At its core, a bank statement mortgage loan allows a borrower to qualify for a mortgage based on the cash flow reflected in their bank accounts rather than the income reported on their tax returns. This distinction is critical. Many self-employed individuals use legitimate business deductions to reduce their taxable income, which can make them appear less qualified on paper than they actually are. For example, a borrower may generate substantial revenue through their business but show minimal net income after expenses on their tax returns. Traditional lenders will typically base their decision on that reduced taxable income, often resulting in a denial or a significantly lower loan amount. Bank statement programs, on the other hand, focus on actual deposits and cash flow, offering a more accurate representation of the borrower's financial capacity.

The origin of bank statement lending can be traced back to the broader category of Non-QM (non-qualified mortgage) loans, which are designed for borrowers who do not meet the strict guidelines of conventional, FHA, VA, or USDA loan programs. Following the financial crisis, lending standards became more rigid, and many borrowers with strong financial profiles found themselves unable to qualify under traditional guidelines. In response, lenders and investors began developing alternative programs that could responsibly serve these borrowers while still managing risk. Bank statement loans became one of the most widely used and effective solutions within this space.

Understanding why these loans exist requires a deeper look at how income is structured for self-employed borrowers. Unlike W-2 employees who receive consistent paychecks with taxes already withheld, self-employed individuals often have fluctuating income streams. They may receive payments from multiple clients, reinvest profits into their businesses, and strategically manage expenses to optimize tax outcomes. While these practices are financially sound, they can create challenges when it comes to traditional underwriting. A tax return might show a lower income figure due to deductions such as equipment purchases, business travel, marketing expenses, and other write-offs. However, these deductions do not necessarily reflect a lack of cash flow. In many cases, the borrower's actual financial position is much stronger than what the tax return suggests.

Bank statement mortgage loans address this issue by shifting the focus from taxable income to gross deposits. Lenders review bank statements over a specified period—typically 12 or 24 months—to calculate an average monthly income. This process involves analyzing all eligible deposits, excluding non-income items such as transfers, refunds, or one-time anomalies. The lender may then apply an expense factor, especially for business accounts, to estimate net income. For example, if a borrower has $20,000 in average monthly deposits and the lender applies a 50% expense factor, the qualifying income would be $10,000 per month. This approach allows lenders to account for business expenses while still recognizing the borrower's overall earning power.

Another reason bank statement loans exist is to provide flexibility in a lending environment that is increasingly diverse. Today's borrowers include gig economy workers, real estate investors, consultants, freelancers, and professionals who operate outside the traditional employment model. These individuals often have strong earning potential and significant assets, but their income documentation does not fit neatly into conventional guidelines. Bank statement programs are designed to accommodate these profiles, offering a pathway to homeownership and investment that would otherwise be inaccessible.

It is important to understand that while bank statement loans offer flexibility, they are not a shortcut or a loophole. Lenders still perform a thorough evaluation of the borrower's financial profile, including credit history, assets, reserves, and overall risk. In many cases, these loans require higher credit scores, larger down payments, and more reserves than traditional loans. This is because the lender is taking on additional risk by using alternative documentation. As a result, borrowers must demonstrate strength in other areas to offset that risk.

One of the key advantages of bank statement mortgage loans is their ability to align with real-world financial behavior. Instead of forcing borrowers to conform to a rigid documentation model, these programs adapt to how people actually earn and manage money. This alignment creates opportunities for borrowers who might otherwise be overlooked by traditional lenders. It also empowers borrowers to take control of their financial narrative by presenting their income in a way that accurately reflects their situation.

As you continue through this chapter, it is essential to recognize that bank statement loans are not just a product—they are a strategy. Successfully qualifying for one of these loans often requires careful planning, organization, and an understanding of how lenders interpret financial data. Borrowers who approach the process strategically, with clean and consistent bank statements, clear documentation, and a well-structured financial profile, are far more likely to achieve favorable outcomes.

In addition, the existence of bank statement loans reflects a broader trend in the financial industry toward personalization and flexibility. As technology advances and data analysis becomes more sophisticated, lenders are increasingly able to evaluate borrowers using a wider range of information. This evolution is creating new opportunities for borrowers to access financing in ways that were not possible in the past. Bank statement loans are at the forefront of this movement, offering a practical and effective solution for a growing segment of the population. Ultimately, the purpose of bank statement mortgage loans is to bridge the gap between traditional underwriting and modern income realities. They provide a way for borrowers to leverage their true earning power, even if it is not fully captured on a tax return. By understanding how these loans work and why they exist, you are taking the first step toward unlocking a powerful tool that can help you achieve your real estate and financial goals.

Real-Life Math Example: How a Borrower Qualifies Using Bank Statements

To fully understand how bank statement mortgage loans work in practice, it is important to walk through a detailed real-life example that illustrates how income is calculated and how a borrower qualifies. Consider a self-employed borrower named Daniel, who owns a digital marketing agency. Daniel has been in business for five years and generates consistent revenue from multiple clients. However, like many business owners, he takes advantage of tax deductions to reduce his taxable income. As a result, his tax returns show a net income of only $70,000 per year, even though his business generates significantly more cash flow.

Daniel wants to purchase a home and applies for a traditional mortgage. Based on his tax returns, the lender calculates his monthly income at approximately $5,833. After factoring in his existing debts, the lender determines that he qualifies for a much smaller loan than he needs. Frustrated by this limitation, Daniel explores alternative options and learns about bank statement mortgage loans.

Daniel decides to apply for a bank statement loan using 12 months of business bank statements. Over the past year, his business account shows the following total monthly deposits: January $18,000, February $20,000, March $22,000, April $19,000, May $21,000, June $23,000, July $24,000, August $22,000, September $21,000, October $23,000, November $25,000, and December $26,000. When these amounts are added together, the total annual deposits equal $264,000. To determine his average monthly income, the lender divides this total by 12, resulting in $22,000 per month in gross deposits.

Next, the lender applies an expense factor to account for Daniel's business costs. In this case, the lender uses a 50% expense ratio, which is common for many industries. This means that half of Daniel's deposits are assumed to go toward business expenses, leaving the other half as qualifying income. After applying this factor, Daniel's monthly qualifying income is calculated as $11,000.

Now, compare this to the $5,833 monthly income derived from his tax returns. By using bank statements, Daniel's qualifying income has nearly doubled. This significant increase allows him to qualify for a much larger loan amount. For example, if the lender allows a debt-to-income ratio of 50%, Daniel can now support total monthly obligations of up to $5,500. After subtracting his existing debts, he has enough capacity to afford a mortgage payment that aligns with his desired home purchase.

In addition to income, the lender also evaluates Daniel's credit score, which is 720, his down payment of 20%, and his reserves, which cover six months of mortgage payments. These strong compensating factors further support his application and help mitigate the risk associated with alternative documentation. As a result, Daniel is approved for the loan and is able to purchase his home.

Now consider how the outcome might differ if Daniel used a 24-month program instead of a 12-month program. If his income had been less consistent in the earlier months, the 24-month average might be lower, reducing his qualifying income. However, if his income had been steadily increasing, the 12-month program would better reflect his current earning power. This example highlights the importance of choosing the right program based on the borrower's financial trajectory.

Another variation to consider is the use of personal bank statements instead of business bank statements. If Daniel regularly transfers funds from his business account to his personal account, the lender might analyze his personal deposits instead. In this case, the expense factor might be lower or even eliminated, depending on the program, which could further increase his qualifying income. However, this approach requires clean and consistent transfers, as well as clear documentation to avoid confusion during underwriting.

It is also important to account for excluded deposits. During the review process, the lender will remove any non-income deposits such as transfers between accounts, loan proceeds, or one-time large deposits that cannot be verified as recurring income. For example, if Daniel received a $50,000 deposit from a one-time project that is not expected to continue, the lender may exclude it from the calculation. This ensures that the qualifying income reflects sustainable cash flow rather than temporary spikes.

Let's take the analysis one step further by calculating a potential loan scenario. Assume Daniel is purchasing a home for $800,000 with a 20% down payment, resulting in a loan amount of $640,000. At an interest rate of 7%, the estimated monthly principal and interest payment is approximately $4,256. Adding property taxes, insurance, and other costs, the total monthly housing payment might be around $5,000. With a qualifying income of $11,000 per month, Daniel's housing ratio is approximately 45%, which falls within acceptable guidelines for many bank statement programs. This example demonstrates how bank statement mortgage loans can transform a borrower's ability to qualify. By focusing on actual cash flow rather than taxable income, these programs provide a more accurate and flexible approach to underwriting. However, they also require careful documentation, consistency, and strategic planning to ensure success.

As you can see, the math behind bank statement loans is both straightforward and powerful. By understanding how deposits are calculated, how expense factors are applied, and how qualifying income is determined, you can position yourself to maximize your approval potential. This knowledge is the foundation for everything you will learn in the rest of this series, and it will serve as a valuable tool as you navigate the world of alternative mortgage financing.

Chapter 2

Who Qualifies for Bank Statement Mortgage Loans

Understanding who qualifies for a bank statement mortgage loan is one of the most important steps in mastering this financing strategy. Unlike traditional mortgage programs that rely heavily on standardized income documentation such as W-2s and tax returns, bank statement loans are designed for borrowers whose income is real, consistent, and verifiable—but not easily captured through conventional methods. These programs open the door to a wide range of individuals who would otherwise be excluded from homeownership or real estate investing opportunities due to how their income is structured.

At the center of this borrower profile is the self-employed individual. Self-employed borrowers include business owners, entrepreneurs, consultants, freelancers, and independent contractors who generate income through their own business activities rather than through a traditional employer. These individuals often have significant earning potential, but their tax returns may not reflect their true income due to deductions, reinvestment strategies, and business expenses. For example, a business owner may generate hundreds of thousands of dollars in revenue annually but show a much lower net income after writing off legitimate expenses such as equipment, travel, marketing, and operational costs. Traditional lenders typically use net income from tax returns, which can severely limit borrowing capacity. Bank statement loans provide a solution by focusing on cash flow instead.

Another major group that qualifies for bank statement mortgage loans is 1099 earners. These are individuals who receive income reported on IRS Form 1099 rather than a W-2. This includes real estate agents, sales professionals, insurance agents, gig economy workers, and many others who are compensated based on commissions, contracts, or project-based work. Like self-employed borrowers, 1099 earners often have fluctuating income and may take deductions that reduce their taxable income. However, their bank statements often show consistent deposits that demonstrate their true earning capacity.

Business owners represent a particularly important category within bank statement lending. These borrowers may operate corporations, LLCs, partnerships, or sole proprietorships. Their income is often tied to the performance of their business, and they may choose to retain earnings within the company rather than distribute all profits as personal income. In these cases, traditional underwriting may not fully capture the borrower's financial strength. Bank statement programs allow lenders to evaluate business revenue directly, often applying an expense factor or using a CPA-prepared profit and loss statement to determine qualifying income. This flexibility makes it possible for business owners to leverage their company's success when applying for a mortgage.

Freelancers and gig economy workers also benefit significantly from bank statement loans. In today's digital economy, many individuals earn income through platforms such as consulting, content creation, ridesharing, online marketplaces, and remote services. These income streams can be highly variable and may not fit neatly into traditional documentation requirements. However, when viewed over a 12- or 24-month period, they often show strong and consistent cash flow. Bank statement programs are designed to recognize this pattern and provide a pathway to qualification.

Real estate investors are another key group that can take advantage of bank statement mortgage loans. Many investors have complex financial profiles that include multiple properties, rental income, and business entities. They may also use strategies such as depreciation to reduce taxable income, which can make it difficult to qualify for traditional loans. Bank statement programs allow investors to use their actual cash flow to qualify, often in combination with other methods such as debt service coverage ratio (DSCR) analysis. This flexibility makes it easier to scale a portfolio and take advantage of new investment opportunities.

While bank statement loans are designed for non-traditional income earners, it is important to understand that not everyone automatically qualifies. Lenders still evaluate several key factors to determine eligibility and risk. One of the most important factors is credit score. Most bank statement programs require a minimum credit score, often in the range of 620 to 680 or higher, depending on the lender and the specific program. A higher credit score can lead to better terms, lower interest rates, and increased approval chances.

Another critical factor is the down payment or equity position. Because bank statement loans involve alternative documentation, lenders typically require larger down payments than traditional loans. This may range from 10% to 25% or more, depending on the borrower's profile and the property type. A larger down payment reduces the lender's risk and demonstrates the borrower's financial commitment to the transaction.

Reserves are also an important component of qualification. Reserves refer to the amount of liquid assets a borrower has available after closing, expressed in terms of months of mortgage payments. For example, a lender may require six to twelve months of reserves to ensure that the borrower can continue making payments even if their income fluctuates. Strong reserves can serve as a compensating factor that offsets other risks in the file.

Consistency of income is another key consideration. Lenders want to see stable and predictable cash flow over time. This does not mean that income must be identical every month, but there should be a clear pattern of ongoing deposits that supports the borrower's ability to repay the loan. Large gaps, unexplained fluctuations, or irregular deposits can raise red flags and may require additional documentation or explanation.

Documentation and organization also play a crucial role in qualification. Borrowers must provide complete and accurate bank statements, typically covering 12 or 24 consecutive months. These statements should be free of excessive overdrafts, non-sufficient funds (NSF) charges, or other indicators of financial instability. Clean and well-organized statements make it easier for underwriters to analyze the file and can significantly improve approval chances.

Another important aspect of qualification is the borrower's overall financial profile. This includes factors such as debt-to-income ratio, employment history, business stability, and the type of property being financed. Lenders look at the complete picture to determine whether the borrower represents an acceptable level of risk. Even though bank statement loans are more flexible in terms of income documentation, they still require a strong and well-rounded financial profile.

It is also worth noting that different lenders and investors may have slightly different guidelines for bank statement programs. This means that a borrower who does not qualify with one lender may still be able to qualify with another. Working with a knowledgeable mortgage professional who understands the nuances of these programs can make a significant difference in finding the right fit.

Ultimately, the goal of bank statement mortgage loans is to provide access to financing for borrowers whose income is real but not traditionally documented. These programs recognize the diversity of modern income streams and offer a practical solution for a wide range of individuals. By understanding who qualifies and what lenders are looking for, you can position yourself to take full advantage of this powerful financing tool.

Real-Life Math Example: Evaluating Different Borrower Profiles for Qualification

To fully understand how qualification works for different types of borrowers, let's examine a detailed real-life scenario involving three individuals with different income structures: Maria, a self-employed business owner; James, a 1099 sales professional; and Lisa, a freelance graphic designer. Each borrower wants to purchase a home and is exploring bank statement mortgage loans as an alternative to traditional financing.

Maria owns a small construction company and has been in business for six years. Her company generates strong revenue, but she writes off a significant portion of her expenses, resulting in a relatively low taxable income. Over the past 12 months, her business bank statements show the following monthly deposits: $30,000, $28,000, $32,000, $35,000, $33,000, $31,000, $34,000, $36,000, $35,000, $37,000, $38,000, and $40,000. The total deposits for the year equal $409,000. Dividing this by 12 results in an average monthly deposit of approximately $34,083.

The lender applies a 50% expense factor to account for business costs, resulting in a qualifying income of $17,041 per month. Maria has a credit score of 740, a 20% down payment, and reserves equal to eight months of mortgage payments.

Based on her strong profile, she is approved for a loan that supports a monthly housing payment of up to $8,500, assuming a debt-to-income ratio of 50%. James is a 1099 sales professional who earns commission-based income. His personal bank statements show consistent deposits over the past 12 months: $12,000, $14,000, $13,500, $15,000, $16,000, $14,500, $15,500, $17,000, $16,500, $18,000, $19,000, and $20,000. The total deposits equal $191,000, resulting in an average monthly income of $15,917. Because James uses personal bank statements and has minimal business expenses, the lender may apply a lower expense factor or none at all, depending on the program. In this case, the lender uses a 25% expense factor, resulting in a qualifying income of $11,938 per month.

James has a credit score of 700, a 15% down payment, and six months of reserves. Based on these factors, he qualifies for a monthly housing payment of approximately $5,500. This allows him to purchase a home that aligns with his financial goals, even though his tax returns alone would not have supported this level of borrowing.

Lisa is a freelance graphic designer who works with multiple clients and earns income through various online platforms. Her income is less consistent than Maria's or James's, but her bank statements show steady overall growth. Over the past 24 months, her total deposits equal $288,000, resulting in an average monthly income of $12,000. The lender chooses the 24-month program to smooth out fluctuations and applies a 40% expense factor, resulting in a qualifying income of $7,200 per month. Lisa has a credit score of 680, a 10% down payment, and four months of reserves. While her profile is slightly weaker than the others, she still qualifies for a loan with a monthly housing payment of approximately $3,200. The lender may require additional compensating factors, such as a slightly higher interest rate or additional reserves, to offset the risk.

Now let's compare these three borrowers to see how their profiles impact their qualification. Maria, with the highest deposits and strongest compensating factors, qualifies for the largest loan amount. James, with consistent personal deposits and moderate expenses, falls in the middle. Lisa, with more variable income and fewer reserves, qualifies for a smaller loan but still benefits from the flexibility of the bank statement program.

This example highlights several important principles. First, the structure of income matters just as much as the amount. Borrowers who can demonstrate consistent and well-documented cash flow are more likely to achieve strong outcomes. Second, compensating factors such as credit score, down payment, and reserves play a critical role in the approval process. Third, the choice between 12-month and 24-month programs can significantly impact qualifying income and should be carefully considered. Let's take the analysis one step further by examining how changes in expense factors affect qualification. If Maria's lender used a 40% expense factor instead of 50%, her qualifying income would increase to $20,450 per month, allowing her to qualify for an even larger loan. Similarly, if James were able to document lower expenses and reduce his expense factor to 20%, his qualifying income would increase to $12,734 per month. These adjustments demonstrate how strategic positioning and documentation can influence the outcome.

Finally, consider the impact of reserves on approval. If Lisa were able to increase her reserves from four months to eight months, she might qualify for better terms or a higher loan amount, even with the same income. This illustrates the importance of strengthening all aspects of the financial profile, not just income.

Through this detailed example, you can see how different borrower types qualify for bank statement mortgage loans and how lenders evaluate their financial profiles. By understanding these dynamics, you can better position yourself or your clients for success and take full advantage of the opportunities these programs provide.

Chapter 3

12-Month vs 24-Month Bank Statement Programs

One of the most important strategic decisions in bank statement mortgage lending is choosing between a 12-month program and a 24-month program. While both options allow borrowers to qualify using bank statements instead of tax returns, the timeframe used to calculate income can significantly impact the final approval, loan amount, and overall strength of the file. Understanding how and when to use each option is critical for maximizing qualifying income and positioning yourself for the best possible outcome.

At a basic level, the difference between these two programs lies in the number of months of bank statements that the lender reviews. A 12-month program analyzes the most recent 12 consecutive months of deposits, while a 24-month program reviews the most recent 24 consecutive months. The lender then calculates the total deposits over the selected period and divides by the number of months to determine an average monthly income. While this may seem straightforward, the implications of choosing one program over the other can be substantial. The 12-month bank statement program is often the preferred option for borrowers whose income has been increasing or who have experienced strong recent performance. Because it focuses only on the most recent year, it captures the borrower's current earning power without being diluted by older, potentially lower-income periods. This makes it particularly useful for business owners who have recently scaled their operations, professionals who have gained new clients or contracts, or anyone whose income trajectory is trending upward.

For example, a borrower who earned $10,000 per month two years ago but now consistently earns $20,000 per month would benefit significantly from a 12-month program. By focusing on the most recent deposits, the lender can use the higher income level to calculate qualifying income, resulting in a larger loan amount. This can be the difference between qualifying for a modest property and securing a higher-value home or investment.

However, the 12-month program also comes with potential risks. Because it relies on a shorter timeframe, it can be more sensitive to fluctuations, inconsistencies, or anomalies in income. If a borrower has uneven deposits, large gaps, or recent declines in income, the 12-month average may not accurately reflect long-term stability. In these cases, the shorter timeframe can work against the borrower, leading to lower qualifying income or increased scrutiny from the underwriter. This is where the 24-month bank statement program becomes valuable. By analyzing a longer period, the 24-month program smooths out fluctuations and provides a more stable and consistent picture of income. This is particularly beneficial for borrowers with variable or seasonal income, such as those in industries like construction, hospitality, sales, or freelance work. Over a two-year period, highs and lows tend to balance out, resulting in a more reliable average.

The 24-month program is also useful for borrowers who may have experienced a temporary dip in income within the past year. For example, if a business owner had a strong year followed by a slower period due to market conditions, the 12-month average might appear lower than expected. By extending the analysis to 24 months, the lender can incorporate the stronger earlier months, improving the overall average and strengthening the borrower's profile.

Another key consideration when choosing between these programs is consistency. Lenders place a high value on predictable and stable income patterns. A borrower with steady deposits over 24 months is often viewed as less risky than one with sharp increases or decreases over a shorter period. Even if the 12-month average is slightly higher, the 24-month program may still be preferred if it demonstrates greater stability and reduces perceived risk. It is also important to consider how underwriters interpret trends within the bank statements. In a 12-month program, underwriters will closely examine whether income is increasing, stable, or declining. A downward trend can raise concerns and may require additional documentation or explanation. In contrast, a 24-month program allows underwriters to view a broader trend, which can help contextualize short-term fluctuations and provide a more balanced assessment.

The choice between personal and business bank statements can also influence the decision between 12 and 24 months. For borrowers using business bank statements, a longer timeframe may provide a clearer picture of revenue and expense patterns, especially if the business experiences seasonal variations. For borrowers using personal bank statements with consistent transfers, a 12-month program may be sufficient if the deposits are stable and well-documented.

Another factor to consider is documentation and complexity. A 12-month program requires fewer statements, which can simplify the application process and reduce the potential for errors or discrepancies. This can be advantageous for borrowers who want a faster and more streamlined approval. A 24-month program, while more comprehensive, requires additional documentation and may involve more detailed analysis, which can extend the timeline. From a strategic standpoint, the decision between 12 and 24 months should always be based on which option presents the borrower in the strongest possible light. This requires a careful review of the bank statements, identification of trends, and an understanding of how different scenarios will impact qualifying income. In many cases, mortgage professionals will calculate both averages and compare the results before selecting the most advantageous option.

It is also worth noting that some lenders may allow flexibility in switching between programs if needed. For example, if a borrower initially applies using a 12-month program but encounters challenges due to income variability, the lender may allow a switch to a 24-month program to improve the outcome. This flexibility can be a valuable tool in navigating complex scenarios.

Ultimately, the decision between 12-month and 24-month bank statement programs is not just a technical choice—it is a strategic one. It requires a deep understanding of the borrower's financial profile, income patterns, and long-term goals. By selecting the right program, borrowers can maximize their qualifying income, strengthen their application, and increase their chances of approval. As you continuc through this series, you will see how this decision plays a critical role in more advanced scenarios, including refinancing, investment properties, and jumbo loans. Mastering this concept early will give you a significant advantage as you navigate the world of bank statement mortgage lending.

Real-Life Math Example: Comparing 12-Month vs 24-Month Qualification Outcomes

To fully understand the impact of choosing between a 12-month and 24-month bank statement program, let's walk through a detailed real-life example involving a borrower named Alex, who owns an e-commerce business. Alex has experienced significant growth over the past two years, but his income has not been consistent throughout that period. This makes him an ideal candidate for analyzing both program options.

Over the past 24 months, Alex's monthly deposits are as follows. For the first 12 months: $10,000, $11,000, $12,000, $11,500, $12,500, $13,000, $12,000, $13,500, $14,000, $13,500, $14,500, and $15,000. These deposits total $152,500 for the first year. For the most recent 12 months, his business has grown significantly, and his deposits are: $16,000, $17,500, $18,000, $19,000, $20,000, $21,000, $22,000, $23,000, $24,000, $25,000, $26,000, and $28,000. These deposits total $259,500 for the second year.

Let's first calculate Alex's qualifying income using the 12-month program. We take the most recent 12 months of deposits, which total $259,500, and divide by 12. This results in an average monthly deposit of $21,625. The lender then applies a 50% expense factor, resulting in a qualifying income of $10,812 per month.

Now let's calculate the 24-month average. We combine the deposits from both years, which total $412,000, and divide by 24. This results in an average monthly deposit of $17,167. Applying the same 50% expense factor, Alex's qualifying income under the 24-month program is $8,583 per month.

The difference between the two programs is significant. By using the 12-month program, Alex's qualifying income is $10,812 per month, compared to $8,583 per month under the 24-month program. This difference of $2,229 per month can have a major impact on the loan amount he qualifies for.

To illustrate this, let's assume the lender allows a debt-to-income ratio of 50%. Under the 12-month program, Alex can support total monthly obligations of up to $5,406. Under the 24-month program, he can support only $4,292. This difference of $1,114 per month in allowable obligations translates into a substantial difference in purchasing power.

Now let's consider a scenario where Alex's income had recently declined instead of increased. Suppose his most recent 12 months of deposits were lower than the previous year, averaging $14,000 per month instead of $21,625. In this case, the 12-month program would result in a lower qualifying income, while the 24-month program would benefit from the higher deposits in the earlier months. This would make the 24-month program the better option.

Let's also examine the impact of fluctuations. If Alex had several months with unusually high deposits followed by several months with lower deposits, the 12-month average might appear inconsistent. The 24-month program would smooth out these fluctuations, providing a more stable average and potentially improving the underwriter's confidence in the file.

Another important factor is how expense ratios affect the outcome. If Alex is able to document lower business expenses and reduce his expense factor to 40%, his qualifying income under the 12-month program would increase to $12,975 per month, while his 24-month income would increase to $10,300 per month. This demonstrates how combining the right program with the right documentation strategy can significantly enhance the final result.

Finally, let's consider the impact on loan approval. Suppose Alex wants to purchase a property with a monthly housing payment of $5,000. Under the 12-month program, his qualifying income supports this payment comfortably, and he is approved. Under the 24-month program, his lower qualifying income may make it more difficult to meet the lender's requirements, potentially resulting in a denial or the need for a larger down payment.

This example clearly shows that the choice between a 12-month and 24-month bank statement program is not just a technical detail—it is a critical decision that can determine the success of the entire transaction. By carefully analyzing income trends, understanding how averages are calculated, and selecting the program that presents the strongest financial profile, borrowers can significantly improve their chances of approval and maximize their purchasing power.

As you move forward, always remember that the goal is not just to qualify—it is to qualify in the best possible way.

Chapter 4

Personal vs Business Bank Statements

One of the most important distinctions in bank statement mortgage lending is whether a borrower qualifies using personal bank statements or business bank statements. While both approaches fall under the same umbrella of alternative documentation, they are analyzed very differently by lenders and can produce significantly different qualifying income results. Understanding when to use each option—and how to structure your finances accordingly—is a critical skill that can dramatically improve your approval chances and loan terms.

At a high level, personal bank statement programs evaluate deposits into a borrower's personal checking or savings accounts, while business bank statement programs evaluate deposits into a business account owned by the borrower. The key difference lies in how lenders interpret those deposits and how they account for expenses. Personal bank statement programs tend to be simpler and often result in higher qualifying income, while business bank statement programs require more analysis but can be more appropriate for borrowers who keep their income within their business. Personal bank statement loans are generally designed for borrowers who transfer income from their business into their personal accounts on a regular basis. In this scenario, the lender reviews the deposits in the personal account and assumes that these deposits represent usable income. Because the funds have already been transferred from the business, many lenders apply little to no expense factor, or a reduced expense ratio, since business expenses are assumed to have already been accounted for before the transfer.

For example, if a borrower consistently transfers $15,000 per month from their business account into their personal account, a lender may use the full $15,000 as qualifying income or apply a small reduction depending on the program. This can result in significantly higher qualifying income compared to using business bank statements, where a larger expense factor is typically applied.

However, personal bank statement programs require consistency and clarity. The transfers must be regular, well-documented, and clearly tied to business income. Random or irregular transfers can raise red flags during underwriting and may require additional explanation. Lenders want to see a clear pattern that demonstrates stable and ongoing income.

Another important consideration with personal bank statements is the need for clean accounts. Personal accounts should ideally show consistent deposits, minimal overdrafts, and limited non-income transactions that could complicate the analysis. Large unexplained deposits, transfers between accounts, or commingling of funds can create confusion and potentially reduce qualifying income.

On the other hand, business bank statement programs are designed for borrowers who keep their income within their business accounts rather than transferring it to personal accounts. This is common among business owners who reinvest profits, maintain operating capital, or prefer to manage finances at the business level. In these cases, the lender analyzes the total deposits into the business account and applies an expense factor to estimate net income.

The expense factor is a critical component of business bank statement analysis. It represents the percentage of revenue that is assumed to be used for business expenses. This can vary depending on the industry, the lender, and the documentation provided. A common default expense factor is 50%, but it can range from 30% to 70% or more. A lower expense factor results in higher qualifying income, while a higher expense factor reduces the income used for qualification.

In some cases, borrowers can provide additional documentation to reduce the expense factor. For example, a

CPA-prepared profit and loss statement may demonstrate that the business operates with lower expenses than the lender's default assumption. This can allow the lender to use a more favorable expense ratio, increasing the borrower's qualifying income.

Business bank statement programs are often more complex than personal programs because they require a deeper understanding of the borrower's business operations. Lenders may review the type of business, the consistency of revenue, and the nature of deposits to ensure that the income is stable and sustainable. This additional analysis can make the process more detailed, but it also allows for greater flexibility in certain situations.

Choosing between personal and business bank statements is not always straightforward. The best option depends on how the borrower manages their finances, the consistency of their deposits, and the overall strength of their profile. In many cases, mortgage professionals will analyze both options and select the one that produces the highest qualifying income while maintaining a strong and clean file.

For example, a borrower who transfers most of their business income into their personal account on a consistent basis may benefit from using personal bank statements, as this can maximize qualifying income and simplify the analysis. Conversely, a borrower who retains most of their income within the business and does not make regular transfers may be better suited for a business bank statement program.

Another important factor to consider is documentation. Personal bank statement programs typically require fewer supporting documents, making them faster and easier to process. Business bank statement programs, on the other hand, may require additional documentation such as business licenses, CPA letters, or profit and loss statements. While this adds complexity, it can also provide opportunities to strengthen the file and improve the outcome.

It is also important to consider how underwriters view risk. Personal bank statement programs are often perceived as lower risk because the income has already been transferred to the borrower's personal account, making it more accessible for living expenses and mortgage payments. Business bank statement programs may be viewed as slightly higher risk because the income remains within the business and may be subject to operational needs.

Ultimately, the goal is to present the borrower's financial profile in the strongest and most accurate way possible. This requires a strategic approach to choosing between personal and business bank statements, as well as careful preparation of documentation and accounts. Borrowers who understand these dynamics can significantly improve their chances of approval and secure better loan terms.

As you continue through this series, you will see how this decision plays a role in more advanced scenarios, including self-employed borrowers, investment properties, and complex loan structures. Mastering the difference between personal and business bank statements is a foundational skill that will support everything you learn moving forward.

Real-Life Math Example: Comparing Personal vs Business Bank Statement Qualification

To fully understand how personal and business bank statements impact qualification, let's walk through a detailed real-life example involving a borrower named Kevin, who owns a consulting business. Kevin generates strong revenue but manages his finances in a way that allows us to analyze both personal and business bank statement scenarios.

Over the past 12 months, Kevin's business bank account shows the following monthly deposits: $25,000, $27,000, $26,000, $28,000, $30,000, $29,000, $31,000, $32,000, $33,000, $34,000, $35,000, and $36,000. The total deposits for the year equal $366,000. Dividing this by 12 results in an average monthly deposit of $30,500. Using a business bank statement program, the lender applies a 50% expense factor. This results in a qualifying income of $15,250 per month. Based on this income, Kevin can support a certain level of monthly housing payment depending on the lender's debt-to-income guidelines.

Now let's analyze Kevin's personal bank statements. Over the same 12-month period, Kevin consistently transfers funds from his business account to his personal account. His personal deposits are as follows: $18,000, $18,500, $19,000, $19,500, $20,000, $20,500, $21,000, $21,500, $22,000, $22,500, $23,000, and $24,000. The total deposits equal $249,500, resulting in an average monthly deposit of $20,792.

Because these are personal bank statements, the lender applies a lower expense factor of 20%, assuming that business expenses have already been accounted for. This results in a qualifying income of $16,634 per month. In some cases, the lender may even use 100% of the deposits, which would result in a qualifying income of $20,792 per month.

Comparing the two scenarios, Kevin's qualifying income is higher when using personal bank statements, even though the total deposits are lower. This is due to the reduced expense factor. Under the business program, his income is $15,250 per month, while under the personal program, it ranges from

$16,634 to $20,792 per month depending on the expense factor used.

Now let's translate this into purchasing power. Assuming a 50% debt-to-income ratio, Kevin can support monthly obligations of $7,625 using business statements, compared to $8,317 to $10,396 using personal statements. This difference can significantly impact the loan amount he qualifies for and the type of property he can purchase.

Let's also consider a scenario where Kevin does not transfer funds consistently. If his personal account shows irregular deposits, the lender may not be able to use the personal statements effectively. In this case, the business bank statement program becomes the better option, even with a higher expense factor.

Another variation involves reducing the expense factor on the business account. If Kevin provides a CPA-prepared profit and loss statement showing that his actual expenses are only 40%, the lender may adjust the expense factor accordingly. This would increase his qualifying income to $18,300 per month, making the business program more competitive with the personal program.

Finally, consider the impact of account cleanliness. If Kevin's personal account has multiple overdrafts or inconsistent deposits, the lender may view it as higher risk, even if the income is higher. In contrast, a clean and consistent business account may provide a stronger overall profile, leading to a better approval outcome.

This example demonstrates that the choice between personal and business bank statements is not just about numbers—it is about strategy. By understanding how each option is analyzed and how different factors impact qualifying income, borrowers can position themselves to achieve the best possible results.

As you move forward, always evaluate both options carefully and choose the one that presents the strongest, most consistent, and most favorable financial picture.

Chapter 5

Bank Statement Mortgage Loans for Primary Residences

Bank statement mortgage loans are not only powerful tools for investors and business owners—they are also highly effective for individuals seeking to purchase or refinance their primary residence. In fact, one of the most impactful uses of bank statement lending is helping self-employed borrowers and non-traditional earners achieve homeownership. For many of these individuals, traditional mortgage programs create unnecessary barriers due to how income is documented. Bank statement loans remove those barriers by focusing on real cash flow, making it possible to qualify for a primary residence without relying on tax returns.

A primary residence is defined as the home in which the borrower intends to live for the majority of the year. Because of this, lenders often offer more favorable terms for owner-occupied properties compared to second homes or investment properties. These advantages may include lower interest rates, higher allowable loan-to-value (LTV) ratios, and more flexible underwriting guidelines. However, even with these benefits, borrowers using bank statement loans must still meet specific requirements and demonstrate financial stability.

One of the key advantages of using a bank statement loan for a primary residence is the ability to qualify based on actual income rather than taxable income. For self-employed borrowers, this can significantly increase purchasing power. Many business owners reduce their taxable income through deductions, which can limit their ability to qualify under traditional guidelines. By using bank statements, lenders can evaluate the borrower's true earning capacity, often resulting in higher qualifying income and access to better housing options.

Loan-to-value ratio, or LTV, is one of the most important factors in primary residence financing. LTV represents the percentage of the property's value that is being financed through the loan. For example, if a borrower purchases a home for $500,000 and makes a $100,000 down payment, the loan amount is $400,000, resulting in an LTV of 80%. In bank statement programs, LTV limits for primary residences are typically more favorable than for investment properties. Borrowers may be able to secure financing with as little as 10% to 15% down, depending on their credit score, reserves, and overall financial profile.

Credit score also plays a critical role in determining eligibility and loan terms. While bank statement loans are more flexible in terms of income documentation, they still require a strong credit profile to offset the additional risk associated with alternative documentation. Higher credit scores can lead to lower interest rates, higher LTV allowances, and more favorable loan terms. Borrowers with lower credit scores may still qualify, but they may need to provide a larger down payment or additional reserves.

Reserves are another essential component of qualifying for a primary residence using a bank statement loan. Reserves refer to the amount of liquid assets a borrower has available after closing, typically expressed in months of mortgage payments. For example, if a borrower's monthly housing payment is $4,000 and the lender requires six months of reserves, the borrower must have at least $24,000 in liquid assets after closing. Strong reserves provide a safety net for both the borrower and the lender, ensuring that payments can be maintained even if income fluctuates.

Owner-occupied guidelines also include occupancy verification. Lenders must confirm that the borrower intends to live in the property as their primary residence. This may involve reviewing the borrower's current living situation, employment location, and other factors that support the occupancy claim. Misrepresenting occupancy can lead to serious consequences, including loan denial or legal issues, so it is critical to be accurate and transparent. Another important aspect of primary residence financing is debt-to-income ratio, or DTI. DTI measures the borrower's total monthly debt obligations relative to their gross monthly income. In bank statement programs, DTI limits may be more flexible than in traditional loans, often allowing ratios up to 50% or higher depending on the lender and compensating factors. This flexibility can be especially beneficial for borrowers with strong income but higher levels of existing debt.

One of the unique advantages of bank statement loans for primary residences is the ability to tailor the loan structure to the borrower's needs. This may include choosing between fixed-rate and adjustable-rate mortgages, selecting loan terms that align with financial goals, and structuring payments to optimize cash flow. For self-employed borrowers, this level of customization can be particularly valuable, as it allows them to align their mortgage with their business income patterns.

Refinancing a primary residence is another area where bank statement loans can provide significant benefits. Borrowers who initially purchased their home using traditional financing may later find that their income structure has changed, making it difficult to qualify for a refinance using tax returns.

Bank statement loans allow these borrowers to access better terms, lower interest rates, or cash-out equity based on their current cash flow rather than outdated income documentation. It is also important to consider the long-term financial impact of using a bank statement loan for a primary residence. While interest rates may be slightly higher than traditional loans due to the alternative documentation, the ability to qualify for a larger loan or secure a desirable property can outweigh this difference. Additionally, as the borrower's financial situation evolves, there may be opportunities to refinance into a traditional loan in the future.

Another key strategy involves preparing your financial profile in advance. Borrowers who plan ahead can optimize their bank statements, maintain consistent deposits, and ensure that their accounts are clean and well-organized. This proactive approach can significantly improve approval chances and lead to better loan terms. For example, avoiding large unexplained deposits, minimizing overdrafts, and maintaining steady income patterns can all contribute to a stronger application.

Ultimately, bank statement mortgage loans for primary residences provide a powerful pathway to homeownership for borrowers who do not fit into traditional lending models. By understanding the key components of qualification—such as LTV, credit score, reserves, and DTI—you can position yourself to take full advantage of these programs and achieve your homeownership goals.

Real-Life Math Example: Qualifying for a Primary Residence Using Bank Statements

To illustrate how bank statement mortgage loans work for primary residences, let's walk through a detailed real-life example involving a borrower named Sophia, who is a self-employed interior designer. Sophia has been in business for four years and generates consistent income, but her tax returns show a lower net income due to business deductions. She wants to purchase a primary residence and decides to use a bank statement loan to qualify.

Over the past 12 months, Sophia's personal bank statements show the following deposits: $14,000, $15,000, $16,000, $15,500, $17,000, $18,000, $17,500, $19,000, $20,000, $21,000, $22,000, and $23,000. The total deposits equal $218,000. Dividing this by 12 results in an average monthly income of $18,167.

Because Sophia is using personal bank statements and has already accounted for business expenses before transferring funds, the lender applies a modest expense factor of 20%. This results in a qualifying income of $14,534 per month. In some programs, the lender may use 100% of the deposits, which would result in a higher qualifying income, but we will use the conservative estimate for this example. Next, we calculate Sophia's maximum allowable monthly debt based on a 50% debt-to-income ratio. With a qualifying income of $14,534, her maximum total monthly obligations are $7,267. Sophia has existing debts totaling $1,200 per month, including a car payment and credit cards. Subtracting this from her maximum allowable obligations leaves $6,067 available for her housing payment.

Now let's determine what home price Sophia can afford. Assume an interest rate of 7% on a 30-year fixed mortgage. A monthly housing payment of $6,067 can support a loan amount of approximately $900,000 when factoring in principal, interest, taxes, and insurance. If Sophia makes a 15% down payment, she can purchase a home priced at approximately $1,058,000.

Next, we evaluate Sophia's reserves. With a monthly housing payment of $6,067, and a lender requirement of six months of reserves, she needs at least $36,402 in liquid assets after closing. Sophia has $80,000 in savings, which comfortably meets this requirement.

Now let's consider how changes in her profile would impact the outcome. If Sophia's credit score were higher, she might qualify for a lower interest rate, which would increase her purchasing power. Conversely, if her credit score were lower, she might need to increase her down payment or accept a higher interest rate, reducing the loan amount she can afford.

Let's also examine the impact of using a 24-month program instead of a 12-month program. If Sophia's income was lower in the previous year, the 24-month average might reduce her qualifying income. For example, if her average over 24 months drops to $15,000 per month, her qualifying income after the expense factor would be $12,000, reducing her maximum housing payment and overall purchasing power.

Another variation involves using business bank statements instead of personal statements. If Sophia's business deposits average $25,000 per month and the lender applies a 50% expense factor, her qualifying income would be $12,500 per month. This is lower than the $14,534 calculated using personal statements, demonstrating why personal statements may be the better option in her case.

Finally, let's consider a refinance scenario. If Sophia already owns a home and wants to refinance to access equity, the same income calculations would apply. With a qualifying income of $14,534 per month, she could potentially refinance into a lower rate or take cash out, depending on her equity and loan terms.

This example demonstrates how bank statement mortgage loans can be used to qualify for a primary residence, even when traditional documentation falls short. By understanding the math behind income calculation, debt-to-income ratios, and loan structuring, borrowers can make informed decisions and maximize their opportunities for approval.

As you continue through this series, you will build on these concepts and learn how to apply them to more advanced scenarios, including investment properties, jumbo loans, and complex financial structures.

Chapter 6

Bank Statement Mortgage Loans for Investment Properties

Bank statement mortgage loans are not only a powerful tool for primary residences—they are one of the most strategic financing methods available for building and scaling an investment property portfolio. For real estate investors, especially those who are self-employed or operate through multiple entities, traditional mortgage guidelines can quickly become restrictive. Tax returns often understate true income due to depreciation, write-offs, and reinvestment strategies, making it difficult to qualify for additional loans. Bank statement mortgage loans solve this problem by focusing on actual cash flow, allowing investors to continue growing their portfolios without being limited by how income is reported on paper.

Investment properties are defined as properties that are not owner-occupied and are typically used to generate rental income or long-term appreciation. Because these properties are considered higher risk than primary residences, lenders apply stricter guidelines. This includes lower maximum loan-to-value ratios, higher credit score requirements, and more substantial reserve requirements. However, despite these stricter standards, bank statement loans provide a level of flexibility that is unmatched by traditional financing, making them an essential tool for serious investors.

One of the key advantages of using bank statement loans for investment properties is the ability to qualify based on business or personal cash flow rather than taxable income. Many real estate investors intentionally reduce their taxable income through depreciation and other strategies to minimize taxes. While this is financially beneficial, it can significantly limit borrowing capacity under traditional underwriting. Bank statement programs allow investors to use their actual income—reflected in deposits—to qualify for additional properties, enabling continued portfolio growth.

Another important concept in investment property financing is the integration of bank statement loans with other qualifying methods, particularly debt service coverage ratio (DSCR). DSCR measures the property's ability to generate enough income to cover its debt obligations. In many cases, lenders may allow a combination of borrower income (via bank statements) and property income (via DSCR) to strengthen the overall file. For example, if a property nearly covers its own mortgage payment but falls slightly short, the borrower's bank statement income can bridge the gap, making the deal viable. Loan-to-value ratios for investment properties are typically more conservative than for primary residences. While a primary residence might allow up to 90% LTV in some bank statement programs, investment properties are often capped at 75% to 85% LTV. This means that investors must be prepared to make larger down payments, often ranging from 15% to 25% or more. While this requires more upfront capital, it also reduces risk and can lead to better loan terms.

Credit score is another critical factor in investment property financing. Lenders view investment properties as higher risk because borrowers are more likely to prioritize their primary residence in times of financial stress. As a result, higher credit scores are typically required to qualify for favorable terms. Strong credit not only improves approval chances but can also reduce interest rates and increase allowable LTV.

Reserves play an even more significant role in investment property loans than in primary residence loans. Lenders want to ensure that investors have sufficient liquidity to cover multiple properties, especially in the event of vacancies or unexpected expenses. It is common for lenders to require six to twelve months of reserves for each property owned, including the new property being financed. This means that as an investor's portfolio grows, so does the importance of maintaining strong liquidity. One of the most powerful aspects of bank statement loans for investment properties is the ability to scale. Traditional lending often imposes limits on the number of financed properties a borrower can have, as well as strict debt-to-income requirements that become more restrictive with each additional loan. Bank statement programs, particularly those offered by non-QM lenders, are often more flexible in this regard. This allows investors to continue acquiring properties without being constrained by conventional limits.

Another important consideration is property type. Bank statement loans can be used for a wide range of investment properties, including single-family homes, multi-family properties, short-term rentals such as Airbnb properties, and even mixed-use properties in some cases. Each property type may have specific guidelines and requirements, but the underlying principle remains the same: qualifying based on cash flow rather than tax returns.

Short-term rental properties, in particular, have become increasingly popular among investors. These properties can generate higher income than traditional long-term rentals, but they also come with more variability. Bank statement loans can be especially useful in these scenarios, as they allow investors to use their overall income to qualify, even if the property's income fluctuates. When combined with DSCR analysis or projected rental income, this creates a powerful framework for financing high-performing assets.

It is also important to understand the role of documentation and organization in investment property financing. Lenders will carefully review bank statements, rental agreements, property histories, and other financial documents to assess risk. Clean, consistent, and well-organized documentation can significantly improve approval chances and streamline the underwriting process. Investors who treat their real estate activities as a business—and maintain clear financial records—are far more likely to succeed.

Another strategic advantage of bank statement loans is the ability to separate personal and business finances. Many investors operate through LLCs or other entities, which can provide liability protection and tax benefits. Bank statement programs can accommodate these structures by allowing income to be evaluated at the business level, provided that ownership and control are clearly documented. This flexibility supports more advanced investment strategies and long-term portfolio growth.

Ultimately, bank statement mortgage loans for investment properties are about leverage—leveraging your income, your assets, and your strategy to acquire and manage real estate effectively. By understanding how these loans work and how to position yourself for approval, you can unlock opportunities that would otherwise be unavailable through traditional financing.

As you continue through this series, you will learn how to combine these strategies with advanced structuring techniques, allowing you to build a scalable and sustainable real estate portfolio. The principles you learn here will serve as the foundation for that growth.

Real-Life Math Example: Scaling an Investment Portfolio Using Bank Statement Loans

To fully understand how bank statement mortgage loans can be used for investment properties, let's walk through a detailed real-life example involving an investor named David. David owns a small real estate investment company and has already acquired two rental properties. He now wants to purchase a third property to expand his portfolio, but his tax returns show limited income due to depreciation and write-offs.

Over the past 12 months, David's business bank statements show total deposits of $360,000, resulting in an average monthly deposit of $30,000. The lender applies a 50% expense factor, resulting in a qualifying income of $15,000 per month.

David's existing properties generate rental income, but for this example, we will focus on his bank statement income as the primary qualifying factor. His current monthly debt obligations, including mortgages on his existing properties and other debts, total $7,000. Using a maximum debt-to-income ratio of 50%, David can support total monthly obligations of $7,500. This leaves only $500 available for additional debt, which would not be sufficient for a new property.

However, this is where strategy comes into play. David's lender allows the use of DSCR for the new property. The property he wants to purchase is expected to generate $3,500 per month in rental income, while the projected mortgage payment is $3,000. This results in a DSCR of 1.17, which meets the lender's minimum requirement.

Because the property can support its own debt, the lender may exclude or reduce its impact on David's debt-to-income ratio. This allows David to qualify for the new loan despite his existing obligations. In this scenario, the combination of bank statement income and property income creates a viable path to approval.

Now let's calculate the purchase details. David is buying a property for $400,000 with a 20% down payment, resulting in a loan amount of $320,000. At an interest rate of 7.5%, the monthly principal and interest payment is approximately $2,237. Adding taxes, insurance, and other costs brings the total monthly payment to $3,000. With rental income of $3,500, the property generates positive cash flow of $500 per month. Over a year, this results in $6,000 in additional income, which can be reinvested or used to build reserves.

Next, we evaluate David's reserves. With three properties, each requiring six months of reserves at $3,000 per month, David needs $54,000 in liquid assets. He currently has $80,000 in savings, which satisfies this requirement.

Now let's consider how changes in the expense factor impact the outcome. If David can reduce his expense factor from 50% to 40% by providing a CPA-prepared profit and loss statement, his qualifying income increases to $18,000 per month. This provides additional flexibility and may allow him to qualify for even more properties in the future.

Let's also examine the impact of scaling. If David continues this strategy and acquires two more properties with similar cash flow, he could generate an additional $1,000 per month in net income. Combined with appreciation and potential rent increases, this creates a compounding effect that accelerates wealth building.

Finally, consider a scenario where the property's rental income is lower, resulting in a DSCR below 1.0. In this case, the lender may require David to use more of his personal income to qualify, or he may need to increase his down payment to reduce the loan amount. This highlights the importance of selecting properties that generate strong cash flow.

This example demonstrates how bank statement mortgage loans can be used not just to acquire a single investment property, but to build and scale an entire portfolio. By combining income analysis, DSCR strategies, and careful financial planning, investors can create a sustainable path to long-term wealth.

As you move forward, you will learn how to refine these strategies and apply them to more advanced scenarios, including jumbo loans, refinancing, and complex portfolio structuring.

Chapter 7

Jumbo Bank Statement Mortgage Loans

Jumbo bank statement mortgage loans represent one of the most powerful and strategic tools available for high-income borrowers, business owners, and investors seeking to finance higher-value properties. These loans are specifically designed for situations where the loan amount exceeds conventional conforming loan limits, which are set by agencies such as Fannie Mae and Freddie Mac. When a loan exceeds these limits, it is classified as a jumbo loan, and the underwriting guidelines become more stringent due to the increased risk associated with larger loan balances.

For borrowers using bank statement income, jumbo loans introduce an additional layer of complexity, but they also offer significant opportunities. High-income self-employed individuals, entrepreneurs, and professionals often find themselves in a position where their actual earnings support a luxury home purchase, but their tax returns do not reflect sufficient income to qualify under traditional jumbo guidelines. Bank statement jumbo loans bridge this gap by allowing these borrowers to qualify based on real cash flow rather than taxable income. One of the defining characteristics of jumbo bank statement loans is the higher loan amount.

While conforming loan limits vary by location, jumbo loans typically begin above those thresholds and can extend into the millions of dollars. Because of this, lenders impose stricter requirements to mitigate risk. These requirements often include higher credit score minimums, lower maximum loan-to-value ratios, and more substantial reserve requirements. However, for well-qualified borrowers, these loans provide access to properties that would otherwise be unattainable.

Credit score is one of the most critical factors in jumbo bank statement lending. While standard bank statement loans may allow credit scores in the mid-600s, jumbo programs typically require higher scores, often starting around 700 or 720 and increasing with larger loan amounts. A strong credit profile demonstrates financial responsibility and helps offset the perceived risk of using alternative documentation. Borrowers with excellent credit may also benefit from better interest rates and more favorable terms.

Loan-to-value ratio is another key component. Jumbo bank statement loans generally require larger down payments than their conforming counterparts. While some programs may allow as little as 10% down for smaller loan amounts, it is more common to see requirements of 20% to 30% or more for higher-value properties. This increased equity position reduces the lender's exposure and provides a cushion in the event of market fluctuations.

Reserves are especially important in jumbo lending. Because of the larger loan amounts and higher monthly payments, lenders want to ensure that borrowers have significant financial reserves. It is not uncommon for jumbo bank statement programs to require 12 to 24 months of reserves, depending on the loan size and borrower profile. These reserves must typically be in liquid or easily accessible assets, such as cash, stocks, or retirement accounts.

Another important aspect of jumbo bank statement loans is the concept of compensating factors. Because these loans involve both high loan amounts and alternative income documentation, lenders look for strengths in other areas of the borrower's profile to offset risk. These compensating factors may include a high credit score, significant assets, strong reserves, low debt levels, and a stable business history. The more compensating factors a borrower has, the stronger their application will be.

Income calculation in jumbo bank statement loans follows the same general principles as standard bank statement programs but is often subject to more scrutiny. Lenders carefully analyze deposits, apply expense factors, and evaluate consistency to ensure that the income used for qualification is stable and reliable. In some cases, borrowers may need to provide additional documentation, such as CPA letters or profit and loss statements, to support their income.

Another key consideration in jumbo lending is property type. Jumbo loans are often used to finance luxury homes, high-end primary residences, and premium investment properties. These properties may have unique characteristics, such as custom construction, large acreage, or specialized features, which can affect appraisal and underwriting. Lenders may require more detailed appraisals and additional documentation to ensure that the property supports the loan amount.

Interest rates for jumbo bank statement loans are typically higher than those for conforming loans, reflecting the increased risk associated with larger balances and alternative documentation. However, for borrowers who cannot qualify under traditional guidelines, these loans provide a valuable opportunity to access financing that aligns with their financial reality. Over time, borrowers may have the option to refinance into a lower-rate loan if their documentation or market conditions improve.

Another strategic advantage of jumbo bank statement loans is their flexibility in structuring. Borrowers may have access to a variety of loan options, including fixed-rate mortgages, adjustable-rate mortgages (ARMs), and interest-only loans. Interest-only options, in particular, can be attractive for high-income borrowers who want to maximize cash flow or invest excess capital elsewhere. However, these options require careful planning and a clear understanding of long-term financial implications.

For business owners and entrepreneurs, jumbo bank statement loans can be a powerful tool for aligning personal and business finances. Many high-income individuals generate substantial revenue but choose to retain earnings within their businesses for growth or tax efficiency. Bank statement programs allow these borrowers to leverage their actual cash flow without being penalized for strategic financial decisions.

It is also important to consider the role of financial planning in jumbo lending. Because of the higher stakes involved, borrowers should take a proactive approach to preparing their financial profile. This includes maintaining clean and consistent bank statements, optimizing credit scores, building reserves, and working with experienced professionals who understand the nuances of jumbo bank statement programs. Proper preparation can make the difference between approval and denial, especially in complex scenarios.

Ultimately, jumbo bank statement mortgage loans represent a convergence of opportunity and responsibility. They provide access to high-value properties and significant leverage, but they also require a higher level of financial discipline and strategic planning. For borrowers who understand how to navigate these programs, the rewards can be substantial.

As you continue through this series, you will see how jumbo bank statement loans fit into broader strategies for wealth building, portfolio expansion, and long-term financial growth. Mastering this type of financing will position you to take advantage of opportunities at the highest levels of the real estate market.

Real-Life Math Example: Qualifying for a Jumbo Bank Statement Mortgage Loan

To fully understand how jumbo bank statement mortgage loans work in practice, let's walk through a detailed real-life example involving a borrower named Michael, who owns a successful technology consulting firm. Michael generates significant income through his business, but his tax returns show a lower net income due to deductions and reinvestment. He wants to purchase a luxury primary residence priced at $2,000,000 and plans to use a jumbo bank statement loan to qualify.

Over the past 12 months, Michael's business bank statements show total deposits of $960,000, resulting in an average monthly deposit of $80,000. The lender applies a 50% expense factor, resulting in a qualifying income of $40,000 per month. Because this is a jumbo loan, the lender carefully reviews the consistency of deposits and may require additional documentation to confirm the stability of the business.

Next, we calculate Michael's maximum allowable monthly debt based on a 45% debt-to-income ratio, which is slightly more conservative than standard programs. With a qualifying income of $40,000, his maximum total monthly obligations are $18,000. Michael currently has existing debts totaling $3,000 per month, leaving $15,000 available for his housing payment.

Michael plans to make a 25% down payment on the $2,000,000 property, which equals $500,000. This results in a loan amount of $1,500,000. At an interest rate of 7%, the monthly principal and interest payment is approximately $9,978. Adding property taxes, insurance, and other costs brings the total monthly housing payment to approximately $13,500.

With a maximum allowable housing payment of $15,000, Michael comfortably qualifies for the loan. His strong income, combined with a substantial down payment and manageable debt levels, supports the approval.

Now let's evaluate reserves. With a monthly housing payment of $13,500 and a requirement of 12 months of reserves, Michael needs $162,000 in liquid assets after closing. He currently has $400,000 in savings and investments, which exceeds the requirement and strengthens his application.

Next, consider the impact of adjusting the expense factor. If Michael can provide a CPA-prepared profit and loss statement showing that his actual expenses are 40% instead of 50%, his qualifying income increases to $48,000 per month. This raises his maximum allowable monthly obligations to $21,600, providing additional flexibility and potentially allowing him to qualify for an even higher loan amount or better terms.

Let's also examine a scenario where Michael chooses an interest-only loan. In this case, his monthly payment may be reduced to approximately $8,750 for the interest-only period, significantly increasing his cash flow. This could allow him to invest additional capital into his business or other opportunities. However, he must be prepared for higher payments once the interest-only period ends.

Another variation involves using a 24-month program instead of a 12-month program. If Michael's income was lower in the previous year, the 24-month average might reduce his qualifying income. For example, if his average drops to $70,000 in monthly deposits over 24 months, his qualifying income at a 50% expense factor would be $35,000 per month, potentially impacting his ability to qualify for the full loan amount. Finally, consider the impact of credit score. If Michael's credit score were lower, the lender might require a larger down payment or offer a higher interest rate, increasing his monthly payment and reducing affordability. Conversely, a higher credit score could improve terms and reduce overall costs.

This example demonstrates how jumbo bank statement mortgage loans can be used to finance high-value properties by leveraging real cash flow. By understanding the math behind income calculation, debt ratios, and loan structuring, borrowers can strategically position themselves for approval and maximize their opportunities in the luxury real estate market.

As you continue through this series, you will build on these concepts and learn how to apply them to even more advanced scenarios, including refinancing, credit challenges, and complex financial structures.

Chapter 8

Bank Statement Mortgage Loan Refinancing & Cash-Out Strategies

Bank statement mortgage loans are not only powerful tools for purchasing real estate—they are equally valuable when it comes to refinancing and accessing equity. For self-employed borrowers, business owners, and investors, refinancing can be one of the most strategic financial moves available. Whether the goal is to reduce monthly payments, consolidate debt, improve cash flow, or unlock capital for new investments, bank statement refinancing provides a flexible pathway that aligns with real income rather than tax-reported income.

Refinancing a mortgage involves replacing an existing loan with a new one, typically with different terms. In traditional lending, refinancing often requires updated tax returns and income documentation, which can create challenges for borrowers whose taxable income does not reflect their actual earning capacity. Bank statement refinance programs solve this problem by allowing borrowers to qualify based on deposits and cash flow, making it possible to refinance even if traditional documentation would not support approval. There are two primary types of refinancing strategies in bank statement lending: rate-and-term refinancing and cash-out refinancing. Each serves a different purpose and offers distinct advantages depending on the borrower's goals.

Rate-and-term refinancing focuses on improving the terms of the existing loan without significantly increasing the loan balance. This may involve securing a lower interest rate, switching from an adjustable-rate mortgage to a fixed-rate loan, or extending the loan term to reduce monthly payments. For borrowers whose income has increased or stabilized since their original loan, bank statement programs can provide access to better terms that were previously unavailable.

Cash-out refinancing, on the other hand, allows borrowers to tap into the equity in their property by increasing the loan amount and receiving the difference in cash. This strategy is particularly powerful for investors and entrepreneurs who want to leverage their real estate assets to fund new opportunities. The cash can be used for a wide range of purposes, including purchasing additional properties, investing in a business, paying off high-interest debt, or building financial reserves.

One of the key advantages of using a bank statement loan for refinancing is the ability to qualify based on current cash flow rather than historical tax returns. This is especially beneficial for borrowers who have experienced growth in their business or income but have not yet reflected that growth in their tax filings. By using recent bank statements, lenders can evaluate the borrower's present financial strength and approve a refinance that aligns with their current situation.

Loan-to-value ratio plays a critical role in refinancing, particularly in cash-out scenarios. LTV determines how much equity a borrower can access and how much risk the lender is taking on. For rate-and-term refinances, LTV limits may be relatively high, sometimes up to 90% for primary residences in certain programs. For cash-out refinances, LTV limits are typically lower, often ranging from 70% to 80% depending on the property type, credit score, and borrower profile.

For example, if a borrower owns a home worth $800,000 and has an existing loan balance of $400,000, they have $400,000 in equity. If the lender allows a maximum LTV of 75% for a cash-out refinance, the new loan amount can be up to $600,000. This means the borrower can potentially access $200,000 in cash ($600,000 new loan minus $400,000 existing balance), minus closing costs and fees.

Credit score and reserves remain important factors in refinancing. Borrowers with higher credit scores are more likely to qualify for better terms, while strong reserves provide additional security for the lender. In cash-out scenarios, lenders may be particularly focused on ensuring that the borrower can handle the increased loan balance and monthly payment.

Another important consideration in refinancing is the purpose of the funds. Lenders may evaluate how the borrower plans to use the cash-out proceeds, especially for larger loan amounts. While there are generally few restrictions on how the funds can be used, demonstrating a clear and strategic plan can strengthen the application and improve approval chances.

Debt consolidation is one of the most common uses of cash-out refinancing. By using equity to pay off high-interest debts such as credit cards or personal loans, borrowers can reduce their overall interest costs and simplify their financial obligations. This can also improve cash flow by lowering monthly payments and consolidating multiple debts into a single mortgage payment.

Liquidity strategies are another key benefit of cash-out refinancing. Having access to liquid capital can provide flexibility and security, allowing borrowers to respond to opportunities or challenges as they arise. For business owners, this may include funding expansion, hiring employees, or investing in new ventures. For investors, it may involve acquiring additional properties or improving existing assets.

It is also important to consider the long-term implications of refinancing. While accessing equity can provide immediate benefits, it also increases the loan balance and may extend the repayment period. Borrowers should carefully evaluate the trade-offs and ensure that the refinance aligns with their long-term financial goals. In some cases, it may be beneficial to use a portion of the cash-out funds to improve the property or generate additional income, offsetting the increased debt.

Timing is another critical factor in refinancing. Interest rates, market conditions, and property values can all impact the effectiveness of a refinance. Borrowers who monitor these factors and act strategically can maximize their benefits and minimize costs. For example, refinancing during a period of lower interest rates can significantly reduce monthly payments and overall interest expense.

Another advanced strategy involves using bank statement refinancing in combination with portfolio management. Investors can refinance one property to extract equity and use those funds to acquire additional properties, creating a cycle of growth and reinvestment. This approach requires careful planning and a strong understanding of cash flow, but it can be highly effective for building long-term wealth.

Documentation and preparation remain essential in the

refinancing process. Borrowers should ensure that their bank statements are clean, consistent, and well-organized, with clear patterns of income. Providing additional documentation, such as CPA letters or profit and loss statements, can further strengthen the application and improve the outcome.

Ultimately, bank statement mortgage loan refinancing and cash-out strategies provide a powerful way to unlock the value of real estate assets and align financing with real income. By understanding how these programs work and how to use them strategically, borrowers can take control of their financial future and create opportunities for growth, stability, and success.

Real-Life Math Example: Cash-Out Refinance Strategy Using Bank Statements

To illustrate how bank statement refinancing works in practice, let's walk through a detailed real-life example involving a borrower named Rachel, who owns a primary residence and operates a successful online business. Rachel purchased her home several years ago and has built significant equity due to appreciation and principal reduction. She now wants to access that equity to invest in a new business venture and consolidate high-interest debt.

Rachel's home is currently valued at $900,000, and her existing mortgage balance is $450,000. This means she has $450,000 in equity. She decides to pursue a cash-out refinance using a bank statement loan to qualify based on her business income.

Over the past 12 months, Rachel's personal bank statements show total deposits of $300,000, resulting in an average monthly income of $25,000. The lender applies a 20% expense factor, resulting in a qualifying income of $20,000 per month.

Using a maximum debt-to-income ratio of 50%, Rachel can support total monthly obligations of $10,000. Her current debts, including her existing mortgage and other obligations, total $4,000 per month. This leaves $6,000 available for her new housing payment after refinancing.

Next, we calculate the maximum loan amount based on LTV. The lender allows a maximum LTV of 75% for a cash-out refinance. On a $900,000 property, this results in a maximum loan amount of $675,000. Subtracting the existing balance of $450,000 leaves $225,000 available for cash-out, before closing costs.

Rachel decides to proceed with a new loan of $675,000. At an interest rate of 7%, the monthly principal and interest payment is approximately $4,492. Adding taxes and insurance brings the total monthly housing payment to approximately $5,500, which fits within her allowable limit of $6,000.

After closing, Rachel receives approximately $210,000 in cash after accounting for closing costs. She uses $50,000 to pay off high-interest credit card debt, reducing her monthly obligations by $1,200. She invests $100,000 into her business, which is expected to generate additional income, and keeps the remaining $60,000 as reserves.

Now let's evaluate the impact of this strategy. By consolidating her debt and investing in her business, Rachel improves her overall financial position. Her monthly cash flow increases due to lower debt payments, and her business has the potential to generate additional income, further strengthening her profile.

Let's also consider an alternative scenario. If Rachel's income were lower, say $18,000 per month instead of $25,000, her qualifying income after the expense factor would be $14,400. This would reduce her maximum allowable monthly obligations and potentially limit the loan amount or require a lower cash-out amount.

Another variation involves using a 24-month program. If Rachel's income was lower in the previous year, the 24-month average might reduce her qualifying income, impacting her ability to access the full $225,000. This highlights the importance of choosing the right program based on income trends.

Finally, consider the long-term impact. Rachel has increased her mortgage balance, but she has also improved her liquidity and created opportunities for growth. If her business performs well, she may be able to refinance again in the future under more favorable terms or pay down the loan more quickly.

This example demonstrates how bank statement cash-out refinancing can be used as a strategic tool to unlock equity, improve cash flow, and invest in future opportunities. By understanding the math and planning carefully, borrowers can maximize the benefits of this powerful financing option.

As you continue through this series, you will learn how to apply these strategies to more complex scenarios, including credit challenges and advanced loan structuring.

Chapter 9

Bank Statement Mortgage Loans with Low Credit or Challenges

Bank statement mortgage loans are often viewed as a solution for borrowers with non-traditional income, but they can also be a powerful option for individuals who have experienced credit challenges. Life events such as job loss, medical issues, business downturns, divorce, or unexpected financial hardship can negatively impact credit, even for otherwise strong borrowers. Traditional mortgage programs tend to be rigid when it comes to credit requirements, often resulting in denials for borrowers who fall below specific thresholds. Bank statement loans, particularly within the non-QM space, offer a more flexible approach that considers the full financial picture rather than focusing solely on credit scores.

It is important to understand that low credit does not mean no opportunity. Instead, it means that the loan must be structured more carefully, with stronger compensating factors to offset the perceived risk. Lenders offering bank statement programs with flexible credit guidelines are willing to look beyond the score itself and evaluate the borrower's income, assets, reserves, and overall financial stability. This holistic approach creates opportunities for borrowers who may have been turned away by traditional lenders.

One of the most important concepts in this area is credit event seasoning. Seasoning refers to the amount of time that has passed since a negative credit event, such as a bankruptcy, foreclosure, short sale, or late payment history. Lenders typically require a certain seasoning period before approving a loan, as this demonstrates that the borrower has had time to recover and re-establish financial stability. For example, a borrower who experienced a bankruptcy three years ago but has maintained perfect payment history since may be viewed more favorably than someone with recent delinquencies.

Different types of credit events carry different levels of impact. A foreclosure or bankruptcy may require longer seasoning periods, while isolated late payments or high credit utilization may be easier to overcome. Understanding how lenders evaluate these events allows borrowers to position themselves more effectively and determine the right time to apply for a loan.

Compensating factors play a critical role in overcoming credit challenges. These are strengths in other areas of the borrower's profile that help offset the risk associated with lower credit. Common compensating factors include higher down payments, strong reserves, stable and consistent income, and a low debt-to-income ratio. For example, a borrower with a 620 credit score may still qualify for a bank statement loan if they can provide a 25% down payment, maintain significant reserves, and demonstrate strong cash flow.

Income consistency is particularly important for borrowers with credit challenges. Lenders want to see that the borrower has reliable and predictable income that can support the mortgage payment. Bank statement programs are well-suited for this, as they allow lenders to evaluate actual deposits over time. A borrower with consistent monthly deposits and a clear income pattern can build confidence with the underwriter, even if their credit score is not ideal.

Another key factor is the structure and cleanliness of bank statements. For borrowers with credit challenges, it is especially important to present well-organized and consistent financial records. Excessive overdrafts, non-sufficient funds charges, or irregular deposits can raise concerns and make it more difficult to offset credit risk. Clean bank statements with steady deposits and minimal negative activity can significantly strengthen the application.

Documentation strategies also become more important in these scenarios. Borrowers may need to provide additional explanations or letters of explanation (LOEs) to clarify past credit issues. For example, if a borrower experienced a temporary financial hardship due to a medical emergency, providing documentation and a clear explanation can help the lender understand the context and evaluate the risk more accurately. Transparency and honesty are critical in this process, as lenders are more likely to work with borrowers who provide complete and accurate information.

Loan-to-value ratio is another area where borrowers with credit challenges must be strategic. Lower LTV ratios, achieved through larger down payments, reduce the lender's risk and increase the likelihood of approval. For example, a borrower with a lower credit score may be limited to a maximum LTV of 70% or 75%, requiring a down payment of 25% to 30%. While this requires more upfront capital, it can make the difference between approval and denial.

Interest rates for bank statement loans with credit challenges are typically higher than those for borrowers with strong credit. This reflects the increased risk perceived by the lender. However, it is important to view this as a temporary step rather than a permanent situation. Borrowers can use the loan as a bridge to homeownership or investment, while working to improve their credit over time. Once their credit profile strengthens, they may have the opportunity to refinance into a lower-rate loan.

Another important strategy is focusing on rebuilding credit while preparing for a loan. This includes making on-time payments, reducing credit card balances, avoiding new debt, and monitoring credit reports for errors. Even small improvements in credit score can have a significant impact on loan terms and approval options.

For investors, bank statement loans with flexible credit guidelines can provide opportunities to continue building a portfolio despite past challenges. By combining strong income, strategic property selection, and solid financial management, investors can overcome credit limitations and achieve long-term growth. In some cases, lenders may place more emphasis on the performance of the property itself, particularly when combined with DSCR analysis.

It is also important to work with lenders and mortgage professionals who specialize in non-QM and bank statement programs. These professionals understand the nuances of credit challenges and can help structure the loan in a way that maximizes approval chances. They can also guide borrowers through the documentation process and identify the best programs for their specific situation.

Ultimately, bank statement mortgage loans with low credit or challenges are about opportunity and strategy. They provide a path forward for borrowers who may have experienced setbacks but are now in a position to move forward financially. By understanding how lenders evaluate risk and how to strengthen your profile, you can turn a challenging situation into a successful outcome.

As you continue through this series, you will build on these concepts and learn how to apply advanced structuring techniques to overcome even more complex scenarios. The key is to focus on what you can control—your income, your documentation, and your financial strategy—and use those strengths to achieve your goals.

Real-Life Math Example: Qualifying with Credit Challenges Using Bank Statements

To illustrate how bank statement mortgage loans can work for borrowers with credit challenges, let's walk through a detailed real-life example involving a borrower named Carlos. Carlos is a self-employed contractor who experienced financial difficulties during a market downturn three years ago, resulting in several late payments and a temporary drop in his credit score. Since then, he has rebuilt his business and now generates strong and consistent income, but his credit score remains at 640. Carlos wants to purchase a home priced at $500,000. He decides to apply for a bank statement mortgage loan to qualify based on his income rather than his tax returns.

Over the past 12 months, his business bank statements show total deposits of $240,000, resulting in an average monthly deposit of $20,000. The lender applies a 50% expense factor, resulting in a qualifying income of $10,000 per month.

Using a debt-to-income ratio of 45%, which is slightly more conservative due to his credit profile, Carlos can support total monthly obligations of $4,500. He currently has existing debts totaling $1,000 per month, leaving $3,500 available for his housing payment.

Next, we calculate the loan structure. Due to his credit score, the lender requires a 25% down payment, resulting in a loan-to-value ratio of 75%. On a $500,000 home, this means Carlos must provide a down payment of $125,000, leaving a loan amount of $375,000.

At an interest rate of 8%, which is higher due to his credit profile, the monthly principal and interest payment is approximately $2,751. Adding property taxes, insurance, and other costs brings the total monthly housing payment to approximately $3,400. This fits within his allowable limit of $3,500, allowing him to qualify for the loan.

Now let's evaluate reserves. With a monthly housing payment of $3,400 and a requirement of six months of reserves, Carlos needs at least $20,400 in liquid assets after closing. He has

$50,000 in savings, which meets this requirement and provides additional security for the lender.

Let's consider how improving his credit score would impact the outcome. If Carlos increases his score from 640 to 700, he may qualify for a lower interest rate of 7%. This would reduce his monthly payment to approximately $2,495 for principal and interest, improving affordability and potentially allowing him to qualify for a higher loan amount or reduce his required down payment.

Another variation involves reducing his expense factor. If Carlos provides documentation showing that his business expenses are only 40%, his qualifying income increases to $12,000 per month. This raises his maximum allowable monthly obligations to $5,400, providing more flexibility and potentially allowing him to qualify for a more expensive property.

Now consider a scenario where Carlos had a recent credit event, such as a late payment within the past six months. In this case, the lender may require additional seasoning or impose stricter terms, such as a higher interest rate or larger down payment. This highlights the importance of timing and preparation when applying for a loan. Finally, let's look at the long-term strategy. Carlos uses this loan as a stepping stone to homeownership. Over the next two years, he continues to improve his credit, reduce debt, and maintain strong income. Once his credit score reaches 720, he may be able to refinance into a lower-rate loan, reducing his monthly payment and overall interest cost.

This example demonstrates how bank statement mortgage loans can provide a viable path for borrowers with credit challenges. By focusing on income, compensating factors, and strategic planning, borrowers can overcome obstacles and achieve their financial goals.

As you move forward, remember that credit challenges are not permanent barriers—they are obstacles that can be managed and overcome with the right approach.

Chapter 10

Advanced Bank Statement Mortgage Loan Structuring

Advanced bank statement mortgage loan structuring is where strategy, precision, and financial awareness come together to create approvals that would otherwise seem impossible. At this level, it is no longer just about qualifying—it is about engineering the strongest possible loan scenario using deposits, expense ratios, timing, account structure, and investor guidelines. Borrowers who understand these advanced concepts can dramatically increase their purchasing power, improve loan terms, and position themselves for long-term financial success.

At the core of advanced structuring is the understanding that income is not fixed—it is interpreted. Two borrowers with identical deposits can produce completely different qualifying incomes depending on how those deposits are presented, documented, and analyzed. This is why structuring matters. The goal is to align your financial profile with lender guidelines in a way that maximizes income while minimizing perceived risk. One of the most powerful tools in advanced structuring is deposit optimization. This involves carefully managing how income flows through your accounts to create consistency and clarity. Lenders prefer to see stable, recurring deposits that clearly represent income. Large fluctuations, irregular transfers, or unexplained deposits can reduce qualifying income or trigger additional scrutiny. By creating a predictable pattern of deposits, borrowers can strengthen their profile and improve their approval odds.

Another critical concept is expense ratio strategy. In business bank statement programs, lenders apply an expense factor to estimate net income. However, this factor is not always fixed. Borrowers who provide additional documentation, such as CPA-prepared profit and loss statements, may be able to reduce the expense ratio. For example, lowering the expense factor from 50% to 40% can significantly increase qualifying income. This is one of the most effective ways to improve a loan scenario without increasing actual revenue.

Timing is another key element of advanced structuring. The choice between a 12-month and 24-month program can dramatically impact qualifying income, as discussed in earlier chapters. Beyond that, borrowers can strategically time their application to coincide with periods of higher income, stronger financial performance, or improved credit. For example, delaying an application by a few months to include higher deposits can result in a substantially better outcome. Account structure also plays a major role. Borrowers must decide whether to use personal bank statements, business bank statements, or a combination of both. Each option has its own advantages, and the best choice depends on how income is managed. In some cases, restructuring how funds are transferred between accounts—well in advance of applying—can create a stronger and more favorable income profile.

Another advanced strategy involves layering income sources. Borrowers may have multiple streams of income, such as business revenue, rental income, and investment income. While bank statement programs primarily focus on deposits, some lenders allow additional income sources to be considered if properly documented. Combining these sources can create a more robust financial profile and increase qualifying income.

Debt structuring is equally important. Reducing or restructuring existing debt before applying for a loan can improve the debt-to-income ratio and increase borrowing capacity. This may involve paying down high-interest debt, consolidating loans, or strategically timing new obligations. Even small changes in monthly debt can have a significant impact on qualifying income and loan approval.

Another powerful concept is compensating factor stacking. Instead of relying on a single strength, borrowers can combine multiple positive factors to offset potential weaknesses. For example, a borrower with a slightly lower credit score can strengthen their file by increasing their down payment, building reserves, and demonstrating strong income consistency. When these factors are combined, they create a compelling overall profile that can lead to approval even in challenging scenarios.

Investor guidelines also play a critical role in advanced structuring. Different lenders have different criteria, and understanding these nuances allows borrowers to match their profile with the most suitable program. Some lenders may be more flexible with expense ratios, while others may offer higher LTV limits or more favorable terms for certain property types. Working with knowledgeable professionals who understand these variations can significantly improve outcomes.

Another advanced technique involves scenario modeling. Before submitting a loan application, borrowers or mortgage professionals can run multiple scenarios to determine the best approach. This includes comparing 12-month vs 24-month averages, personal vs business statements, and different expense ratios. By analyzing these scenarios in advance, borrowers can choose the strategy that produces the highest qualifying income and strongest profile.

Cash flow management is also a critical component. Borrowers should not only focus on qualifying for the loan but also on maintaining sustainable cash flow after closing. This includes ensuring that monthly payments are manageable and that sufficient reserves are available to handle unexpected expenses. Advanced structuring is not just about approval—it is about long-term success.

Another key strategy is preparing for future refinancing or portfolio expansion. Borrowers who structure their finances effectively today can create opportunities for better terms or additional loans in the future. For example, maintaining clean bank statements, improving credit, and building reserves can position borrowers for refinancing into lower rates or expanding their real estate portfolio.

It is also important to consider risk management. Advanced structuring should always balance opportunity with caution. Taking on excessive debt or overextending financially can create long-term challenges. Borrowers should carefully evaluate their goals and ensure that their loan structure aligns with their overall financial strategy.

Ultimately, advanced bank statement mortgage loan structuring is about control. It allows borrowers to take control of how their income is presented, how their loan is structured, and how their financial future is shaped. By mastering these techniques, borrowers can unlock opportunities that go far beyond basic qualification.

As this series concludes, you now have a comprehensive understanding of how bank statement mortgage loans work—from fundamentals to advanced strategies. The next step is to apply this knowledge in real-world scenarios, using the principles you have learned to achieve your financial goals.

Real-Life Math Example: Advanced Loan Structuring Scenario

To demonstrate how advanced structuring works in practice, let's walk through a detailed example involving a borrower named Andrew, who owns multiple businesses and is looking to purchase a high-value property while optimizing his loan structure.

Andrew's business bank statements show total deposits of $600,000 over the past 12 months, resulting in an average monthly deposit of $50,000. Using a standard 50% expense factor, his qualifying income would be $25,000 per month. However, Andrew works with a CPA to provide a profit and loss statement showing that his actual expenses are only 40%. This allows the lender to reduce the expense factor, increasing his qualifying income to $30,000 per month.

Next, Andrew evaluates whether to use a 12-month or 24-month program. Over the past 24 months, his total deposits are $1,080,000, resulting in an average monthly deposit of $45,000. With a 40% expense factor, this produces a qualifying income of $27,000 per month. By choosing the 12-month program, Andrew increases his qualifying income by $3,000 per month, which significantly impacts his borrowing capacity.

Andrew also considers using personal bank statements. His personal account shows consistent transfers averaging $35,000 per month. With a reduced expense factor of 20%, his qualifying income would be $28,000 per month. While this is slightly lower than the $30,000 achieved with business statements, the personal statements provide a cleaner and simpler profile, which may improve approval chances.

Now let's calculate Andrew's maximum borrowing capacity. Using a debt-to-income ratio of 50%, his maximum allowable monthly obligations are $15,000 based on a $30,000 monthly income. He has existing debts totaling $3,000 per month, leaving $12,000 available for his housing payment.

Andrew plans to purchase a property for $1,500,000 with a 20% down payment, resulting in a loan amount of $1,200,000. At an interest rate of 7%, the monthly principal and interest payment is approximately $7,984. Adding taxes and insurance brings the total monthly payment to $10,500, which fits within his allowable limit. Now let's examine the impact of debt restructuring. If Andrew pays off a $1,000 monthly obligation before applying, his available housing payment increases to $13,000. This could allow him to qualify for a larger loan or provide additional flexibility in structuring the deal.

Andrew also evaluates reserves. With a monthly payment of $10,500 and a requirement of 12 months of reserves, he needs $126,000 in liquid assets. He currently has $200,000 in savings, which satisfies this requirement and strengthens his application.

Finally, Andrew models different scenarios. If he used the 24-month program with a qualifying income of $27,000, his maximum allowable obligations would drop to $13,500, reducing his available housing payment. This could limit his loan amount or require adjustments to the deal. By choosing the 12-month program and optimizing his expense ratio, Andrew maximizes his borrowing capacity.

This example illustrates how advanced structuring can significantly impact loan outcomes. By optimizing deposits, reducing expense ratios, choosing the right program, and managing debt, Andrew is able to qualify for a high-value property while maintaining a strong financial position. As you apply these strategies, remember that the goal is not just to qualify, but to structure your loan in a way that supports your long-term financial success.

Chapter 11

Common Mistakes to Avoid with Bank Statement Mortgage Loans

As powerful as bank statement mortgage loans are, they require precision, preparation, and strategy. Many borrowers who would otherwise qualify end up facing delays, unfavorable terms, or even denials due to avoidable mistakes. Understanding these pitfalls is essential for anyone looking to successfully navigate this type of financing. In this chapter, we will break down the most common mistakes borrowers make and how to avoid them, so you can position yourself for the strongest possible outcome.

One of the most frequent mistakes is inconsistent or poorly structured deposits. Bank statement loans rely heavily on deposit patterns to determine income. If deposits are irregular, sporadic, or difficult to trace, lenders may not be able to use them for qualification. For example, large deposits that appear without explanation or inconsistent monthly income can create uncertainty for underwriters. The solution is to maintain consistent, traceable deposits that clearly represent income over time. Predictability builds confidence and strengthens your application. Another major mistake is commingling personal and business funds without a clear structure. While many self-employed borrowers use the same accounts for both personal and business expenses, this can complicate the analysis. Lenders need to clearly identify income versus transfers or non-qualifying deposits. When accounts are mixed without documentation, it can lead to reduced qualifying income or additional conditions. A better approach is to maintain separate accounts or ensure that transfers are consistent and well-documented.

Failing to understand expense factors is another common issue. Many borrowers assume that all deposits will count as income, but this is not always the case. In business bank statement programs, lenders apply an expense ratio to estimate net income. If borrowers are unaware of this, they may overestimate their qualifying income and pursue properties beyond their actual approval range. Understanding how expense factors work—and taking steps to reduce them through documentation—can make a significant difference.

Another critical mistake is ignoring the importance of clean bank statements. Overdrafts, non-sufficient funds (NSF) charges, and excessive fees can signal financial instability to lenders. Even if income is strong, these negative indicators can raise concerns and weaken the overall profile. Borrowers should aim to maintain clean accounts with minimal negative activity, especially in the months leading up to a loan application. Timing mistakes are also very common. Applying for a loan during a period of lower income, increased expenses, or recent financial changes can negatively impact qualification. For example, if a borrower has recently experienced a temporary drop in income, using a 12-month program may not produce the best results. Waiting a few months or using a 24-month program could significantly improve the outcome. Strategic timing is often overlooked but can be one of the most powerful tools in bank statement lending.

Another mistake is choosing the wrong program or structure. As discussed in previous chapters, borrowers can often choose between personal and business bank statements, as well as 12-month and 24-month programs. Selecting the wrong combination can reduce qualifying income or create unnecessary complications. It is important to analyze multiple scenarios and choose the option that presents the strongest financial profile.

Overlooking debt-to-income ratio is another issue. Even with strong income, high levels of existing debt can limit borrowing capacity. Some borrowers focus solely on increasing income without addressing their debt obligations. Paying down or restructuring debt before applying can significantly improve the DTI ratio and increase approval chances. This is one of the simplest yet most effective strategies available.

Another common mistake is insufficient reserves. Lenders want to see that borrowers have enough liquid assets to cover mortgage payments in case of income fluctuations. Borrowers who use all of their funds for a down payment without leaving sufficient reserves may face challenges during underwriting. Planning ahead to maintain adequate reserves is essential for a strong application.

Lack of documentation is another major pitfall. Bank statement loans may require additional documentation beyond the statements themselves, such as CPA letters, profit and loss statements, or explanations for unusual deposits. Failing to provide these documents promptly can delay the process or lead to unfavorable outcomes. Being proactive and organized can streamline the process and improve approval chances.

Another mistake is misunderstanding lender guidelines. Not all bank statement programs are the same. Different lenders have different requirements, including varying expense ratios, LTV limits, and credit score thresholds. Assuming that all programs operate identically can lead to missed opportunities or unnecessary denials. Working with experienced professionals who understand these differences can help you find the best fit for your situation. Emotional decision-making is another factor that can lead to mistakes. Some borrowers become focused on a specific property or loan amount and ignore the financial realities of their situation. This can result in overextending financially or choosing unfavorable terms. It is important to approach the process with a clear strategy and realistic expectations.

Another key mistake is failing to plan for the future. Bank statement loans are often used as a stepping stone, with the goal of refinancing into a traditional loan later. Borrowers who do not consider this long-term strategy may miss opportunities to improve their financial position. Maintaining strong financial habits after closing can open the door to better terms in the future.

Communication breakdowns can also create challenges. Delays in responding to lender requests, incomplete information, or misunderstandings can slow down the process and create unnecessary stress. Clear and consistent communication with your mortgage professional is essential for a smooth transaction.

Finally, one of the biggest mistakes is underestimating the importance of preparation. Successful borrowers do not approach bank statement loans casually—they prepare their financial profile months in advance. This includes organizing bank statements, improving credit, reducing debt, and ensuring consistency in income. Preparation is the foundation of success in this type of lending.

By understanding and avoiding these common mistakes, you can significantly improve your chances of approval and secure better loan terms. Bank statement mortgage loans offer incredible flexibility, but they require discipline and strategy to use effectively.

Real-Life Math Example: How Mistakes Impact Loan Qualification

To illustrate how these mistakes can affect loan outcomes, let's examine a detailed real-life example involving a borrower named Jason, who is a self-employed consultant looking to purchase a home.

Jason's business generates strong revenue, and over the past 12 months, his bank statements show total deposits of $300,000, resulting in an average monthly deposit of $25,000. Using a 50% expense factor, his qualifying income is $12,500 per month. Based on a 50% debt-to-income ratio, he can support total monthly obligations of $6,250.

However, Jason makes several mistakes that impact his qualification. First, his bank statements show multiple large deposits that are not clearly documented. These include transfers from other accounts and one-time payments that cannot be verified as recurring income. The lender excludes

$50,000 of these deposits from the calculation, reducing his total deposits to $250,000. This lowers his average monthly deposit to $20,833 and his qualifying income to $10,416 per month.

Next, Jason has several overdrafts and NSF charges on his bank statements. While these do not directly reduce his income, they raise concerns for the underwriter and may require additional reserves or stricter terms. This adds complexity to the approval process.

Jason also has existing debts totaling $2,500 per month. With his reduced qualifying income of $10,416, his maximum allowable obligations at a 50% DTI are $5,208. Subtracting his existing debt leaves only $2,708 available for his housing payment.

Jason initially planned to purchase a home with a monthly payment of $3,500, but due to the reduced qualifying income and higher perceived risk, he no longer qualifies for this amount. He must either choose a less expensive property or improve his financial profile.

Now let's examine how correcting these mistakes would change the outcome. If Jason provides documentation for the excluded deposits and demonstrates that they are legitimate income, his total deposits return to $300,000, and his qualifying income increases back to $12,500 per month. This raises his maximum allowable obligations to $6,250, leaving $3,750 available for housing after accounting for his existing debt.

Additionally, if Jason pays off $1,000 of his monthly debt before applying, his available housing payment increases to $4,750. This significantly improves his purchasing power and allows him to qualify for a higher-priced home.

If Jason also cleans up his bank statements by avoiding overdrafts and maintaining consistent deposits for several months before applying, his overall profile becomes stronger, potentially leading to better loan terms and a smoother approval process.

Finally, consider the impact of choosing the right program. If Jason's income has been increasing, using a 12-month program may produce a higher average than a 24-month program. Conversely, if his income has been inconsistent, the 24-month program may provide a more stable average. Selecting the right option can further improve his qualification.

This example demonstrates how small mistakes can have a significant impact on loan outcomes. By addressing these issues and taking a strategic approach, borrowers can maximize their qualifying income and improve their chances of approval. As you move forward, remember that success in bank statement lending is not just about income—it is about how that income is presented and supported. Avoiding these common mistakes will put you in the best position to achieve your goals.

Chapter 12

The Complete Bank Statement Loan Approval Blueprint

At this point in the Bank Statement Mortgage Loan Mastery Series, you have developed a deep understanding of how these loans work—from income calculation and program selection to advanced structuring and avoiding costly mistakes. Now it is time to bring everything together into a complete, step-by-step blueprint for approval. This chapter is designed to give you a clear, repeatable system that you can follow to successfully qualify for a bank statement mortgage loan, whether for a primary residence, investment property, or refinancing strategy.

The first step in the blueprint is clarity. Before you even begin the application process, you must clearly define your goal. Are you purchasing a primary residence, scaling an investment portfolio, or refinancing to access equity? Each objective may require a slightly different strategy, and understanding your end goal will guide every decision you make. Clarity also includes knowing your target purchase price, desired monthly payment, and long-term financial plan. The second step is financial assessment. This involves taking a detailed look at your current financial situation, including your bank statements, credit score, debts, assets, and reserves. You should calculate your average monthly deposits, estimate your qualifying income based on potential expense factors, and evaluate your debt-to-income ratio. This step allows you to understand where you stand before approaching a lender and helps you identify areas that may need improvement.

The third step is income optimization. This is where you apply many of the strategies discussed throughout this series. You must decide whether to use personal or business bank statements, choose between a 12-month or 24-month program, and ensure that your deposits are consistent and well-documented. If possible, work with a CPA to provide a profit and loss statement that may reduce your expense ratio and increase your qualifying income. This step is about presenting your income in the strongest and most accurate way possible.

The fourth step is credit and debt positioning. Even though bank statement loans focus on income, credit and debt still play a critical role. You should review your credit report, address any errors, and take steps to improve your score if needed. At the same time, evaluate your existing debt and consider paying down or restructuring obligations to improve your debt-to-income ratio. Small improvements in this area can have a significant impact on your approval and loan terms.

The fifth step is reserve building. Lenders want to see that you have sufficient liquidity to handle mortgage payments and unexpected expenses. You should ensure that you have enough reserves to meet lender requirements, which may range from six to twelve months of mortgage payments or more. Strong reserves not only improve approval chances but also provide financial security after closing.

The sixth step is documentation preparation. This is one of the most critical parts of the process. You should gather all required documents in advance, including bank statements, identification, business documentation, and any additional supporting materials such as CPA letters or explanations for unusual deposits. Organized and complete documentation can significantly speed up the approval process and reduce the likelihood of delays or conditions.

The seventh step is lender and program selection. Not all lenders offer the same bank statement programs, and guidelines can vary significantly. It is important to work with a knowledgeable mortgage professional who understands the nuances of these programs and can match you with the best lender for your situation. Choosing the right program can make a substantial difference in your approval and loan terms.

The eighth step is scenario modeling. Before submitting your application, you should evaluate multiple scenarios to determine the best approach. This includes comparing different income calculations, program options, and loan structures. By modeling these scenarios in advance, you can choose the strategy that maximizes your qualifying income and minimizes risk.

The ninth step is application execution. Once you have prepared your financial profile and selected the right program, you can move forward with the application. This step requires accuracy, transparency, and attention to detail. Provide all requested information promptly and ensure that your application reflects your financial situation accurately.

The tenth step is underwriting navigation. During underwriting, the lender will review your file in detail and may request additional documentation or clarification. This is a normal part of the process. Responding quickly and providing clear, complete information can help move your file through underwriting efficiently. Staying proactive and engaged during this stage is essential.

The eleventh step is final approval and closing preparation. Once your loan is approved, you will move toward closing. This includes reviewing final loan terms, ensuring that all conditions are met, and preparing for closing costs and down payment requirements. Understanding the final structure of your loan is critical to ensuring that it aligns with your financial goals.

The twelfth and final step is post-closing strategy. Approval is not the end of the journey—it is the beginning. After closing, you should focus on maintaining strong financial habits, improving your credit, and preparing for future opportunities. This may include refinancing into a lower-rate loan, acquiring additional properties, or using your equity strategically.

One of the most important principles of this blueprint is consistency. Every step builds on the previous one, and success comes from executing each step with precision and discipline. Borrowers who follow this process systematically are far more likely to achieve successful outcomes than those who approach the process without a clear plan.

Another key principle is adaptability. Every borrower's situation is unique, and the blueprint must be tailored to fit individual circumstances. This may involve adjusting strategies based on income patterns, credit profile, or market conditions. Flexibility and awareness are essential for navigating complex scenarios.

This blueprint is not just a checklist—it is a framework for success. It empowers you to take control of the process, understand how lenders evaluate your profile, and position yourself for the best possible outcome. Whether you are a first-time borrower or an experienced investor, this system can be applied repeatedly to achieve consistent results.

As you complete this series, you now have the knowledge and tools to navigate the world of bank statement mortgage loans with confidence. The next step is to apply this blueprint in real-world scenarios and take action toward your financial goals.

Real-Life Math Example: Applying the Complete Approval Blueprint

To bring this blueprint to life, let's walk through a comprehensive real-life example involving a borrower named Elena, who is a self-employed marketing consultant looking to purchase a home using a bank statement mortgage loan.

Elena's goal is to purchase a home priced at $700,000. She begins by assessing her financial situation. Over the past 12 months, her personal bank statements show total deposits of $360,000, resulting in an average monthly income of $30,000. The lender applies a 20% expense factor, resulting in a qualifying income of $24,000 per month.

Next, Elena calculates her debt-to-income ratio. Using a maximum DTI of 50%, she can support total monthly obligations of $12,000. She currently has existing debts totaling $2,000 per month, leaving $10,000 available for her housing payment.

Elena then evaluates her loan structure. She plans to make a 15% down payment, which equals $105,000. This results in a loan amount of $595,000. At an interest rate of 7%, her monthly principal and interest payment is approximately $3,959. Adding taxes and insurance brings the total monthly housing payment to approximately $4,800, which is well within her allowable limit of $10,000.

Next, Elena reviews her reserves. With a monthly housing payment of $4,800 and a requirement of six months of reserves, she needs at least $28,800 in liquid assets after closing. She has $90,000 in savings, which comfortably meets this requirement.

Now let's apply advanced structuring strategies. Elena considers using a 24-month program, but her income was lower in the previous year, resulting in an average monthly deposit of $25,000. After applying the expense factor, her qualifying income would drop to $20,000 per month, reducing her maximum allowable obligations. By choosing the 12-month program, she maximizes her income and improves her approval scenario.

Elena also evaluates her expense factor. By working with a CPA to provide a profit and loss statement, she demonstrates that her actual expenses are only 15%. This increases her qualifying income to $25,500 per month, further strengthening her profile.

Next, Elena reviews her debt and decides to pay off a $500 monthly obligation before applying. This increases her available housing payment and provides additional flexibility.

Now let's consider the final outcome. With a qualifying income of $25,500 per month and reduced debt, Elena's maximum allowable obligations increase to $12,750. After subtracting her remaining debt, she has over $10,000 available for housing, far exceeding her required payment of $4,800.

Finally, Elena completes the application process, provides all required documentation, and successfully navigates underwriting. Her strong income, clean bank statements, solid reserves, and strategic preparation result in a smooth approval and closing.

This example demonstrates how the complete blueprint can be applied to achieve a successful outcome. By following each step—clarity, assessment, optimization, and execution—Elena is able to maximize her qualifying income, secure favorable terms, and achieve her homeownership goal.

As you apply this blueprint to your own situation, remember that preparation, strategy, and consistency are the keys to success. With the knowledge you have gained throughout this series, you are now equipped to navigate bank statement mortgage loans with confidence and precision.

Chapter 13

Scaling Wealth with Bank Statement Mortgage Loans

Bank statement mortgage loans are not just a solution for getting approved—they are a long-term wealth-building strategy. When used correctly, these loans allow self-employed borrowers, entrepreneurs, and investors to break free from traditional income limitations and scale real estate holdings in a way that compounds over time. This chapter focuses on how to use bank statement loans strategically to build, expand, and sustain wealth through real estate and cash flow optimization.

At the highest level, wealth creation with bank statement loans revolves around one concept: leverage. Leverage allows you to control high-value assets using a relatively small amount of your own capital. By using bank statement loans, you can qualify based on real income and access financing that reflects your true earning power. This opens the door to acquiring more properties, increasing cash flow, and benefiting from long-term appreciation.

The first principle of scaling wealth is understanding the difference between income and cash flow. Many borrowers focus solely on income, but true wealth is built through cash flow—money that remains after expenses. Bank statement loans allow you to qualify using income, but your goal should be to acquire assets that generate positive cash flow. This creates a self-sustaining system where your properties help fund future investments.

Another key principle is velocity of capital. This refers to how quickly you can deploy and redeploy your capital into new opportunities. Bank statement loans, especially when combined with refinancing strategies, allow you to recycle your capital. For example, you can purchase a property, increase its value, refinance to extract equity, and then use that equity to acquire another property. This cycle can be repeated over time, accelerating wealth creation.

Portfolio scaling is the next level of this strategy. Instead of focusing on a single property, you begin to think in terms of a portfolio of assets. Each property contributes to your overall financial picture through rental income, appreciation, and tax benefits. Bank statement loans make it possible to continue acquiring properties even when traditional lending would limit your ability to qualify due to tax return constraints.

One of the most effective strategies for scaling is combining bank statement loans with debt service coverage ratio (DSCR) loans. While bank statement loans focus on your personal or business income, DSCR loans focus on the income generated by the property itself. By using both strategies together, you can qualify for more deals and create a balanced portfolio that leverages both personal income and property performance.

Another important concept is diversification. As your portfolio grows, it is important to diversify across property types, locations, and income streams. This reduces risk and creates multiple sources of income. For example, you might own a mix of long-term rentals, short-term rentals, and multi-family properties. Bank statement loans provide the flexibility to finance a wide range of property types, supporting this diversification strategy.

Risk management is also critical when scaling wealth. While leverage can accelerate growth, it also increases exposure. Borrowers must ensure that their properties generate sufficient cash flow and that they maintain adequate reserves. This includes planning for vacancies, maintenance, and market fluctuations. Strong financial discipline is essential for sustaining long-term growth.

Another key strategy is optimizing loan structures. As you acquire more properties, the structure of your loans becomes increasingly important. This includes choosing between fixed and adjustable rates, managing interest-only periods, and aligning loan terms with your investment strategy. Bank statement loans offer flexibility in structuring, allowing you to tailor your financing to your goals.

Tax strategy also plays a significant role in wealth building. Real estate investors often benefit from deductions such as depreciation, which can reduce taxable income. While this can limit qualification under traditional lending, bank statement loans allow you to continue leveraging your real income. Working with a knowledgeable tax professional can help you optimize your strategy and maximize your returns.

Another powerful concept is compounding. As you reinvest cash flow and equity into new properties, your portfolio begins to grow exponentially. Each new acquisition adds to your income and increases your overall asset base. Over time, this creates a snowball effect that accelerates wealth creation.

Timing the market is less important than consistency. Many successful investors focus on acquiring properties consistently over time rather than trying to predict market movements. Bank statement loans support this approach by providing ongoing access to financing, allowing you to act on opportunities as they arise.

Another advanced strategy is using refinancing as a growth tool. By refinancing properties as they appreciate, you can extract equity and reinvest it into new deals. This allows you to grow your portfolio without relying solely on new capital. Bank statement refinance programs make this possible even for borrowers with non-traditional income.

Building a team is also an important part of scaling wealth. This includes working with mortgage professionals, real estate agents, accountants, and property managers who understand your strategy. A strong team can help you identify opportunities, structure deals, and manage your portfolio effectively.

Long-term vision is essential. Scaling wealth with bank statement loans is not about quick wins—it is about building a sustainable system that generates income and appreciation over time. This requires patience, discipline, and a clear strategy.

Ultimately, bank statement mortgage loans provide a pathway to financial independence for those who understand how to use them strategically. By leveraging income, optimizing cash flow, and reinvesting profits, you can build a portfolio that supports your long-term goals and creates lasting wealth.

Real-Life Math Example: Scaling a Real Estate Portfolio Using Bank Statement Loans

To demonstrate how bank statement loans can be used to scale wealth, let's walk through a detailed example involving a borrower named Marcus, who is a self-employed entrepreneur with a growing real estate portfolio.

Marcus starts with a business that generates $40,000 per month in deposits, based on his bank statements. Using a 50% expense factor, his qualifying income is $20,000 per month. With a 50% debt-to-income ratio, he can support total monthly obligations of $10,000.

Marcus purchases his first investment property for $300,000 with a 20% down payment, resulting in a loan amount of $240,000. His monthly payment, including taxes and insurance, is $2,000. The property generates $2,500 in rental income, creating $500 in positive cash flow.

After one year, Marcus's business grows, and his deposits increase to $50,000 per month. His qualifying income rises to $25,000 per month, allowing him to support higher debt levels. He uses a bank statement loan to purchase a second property for $350,000 with similar cash flow.

Now Marcus owns two properties generating a combined $1,000 in monthly cash flow. He continues to reinvest this income while his properties appreciate in value. After two years, his first property is worth $360,000, and his second property is worth $420,000. Marcus decides to refinance his first property. With an 80% loan-to-value ratio, he can refinance up to $288,000. His existing loan balance is $230,000, allowing him to extract $58,000 in cash. He uses this money as a down payment for a third property.

With three properties, Marcus's monthly cash flow increases to $1,500. His business income continues to grow, and his bank statement deposits now average $60,000 per month. His qualifying income is $30,000 per month, allowing him to support even more debt.

Marcus repeats this process, acquiring additional properties over time. Each property contributes to his cash flow and increases his overall net worth. By year five, he owns six properties generating $3,000 per month in cash flow, in addition to his business income.

Let's analyze the numbers. Marcus's total property value is now approximately $2,000,000, with loan balances totaling $1,400,000. This gives him $600,000 in equity. His monthly cash flow of $3,000 adds up to $36,000 per year, which he can reinvest or use for other purposes.

If Marcus continues this strategy for another five years, his portfolio could double in size, with even greater cash flow and equity. This demonstrates the power of compounding and leverage when combined with bank statement loans. Now consider how changes in strategy impact the outcome. If Marcus reduces his expense factor to 40% by providing better documentation, his qualifying income increases, allowing him to acquire properties more quickly. If he improves his credit score, he may secure better loan terms, increasing cash flow.

This example shows how bank statement loans can be used as a foundation for scaling wealth. By combining income growth, strategic financing, and reinvestment, borrowers can build a portfolio that generates long-term income and financial freedom.

As you apply these principles, remember that consistency and discipline are key. Wealth is not built overnight—it is built through repeated, strategic actions over time.

Chapter 14

Long-Term Exit Strategies & Financial Freedom with Bank Statement Loans

As you reach this stage of the Bank Statement Mortgage Loan Mastery Series, the focus shifts from acquisition and growth to long-term strategy, exit planning, and financial freedom. While many borrowers initially use bank statement loans to qualify for a home or investment property, the most successful individuals think several steps ahead. They understand that every loan, every property, and every financial decision should align with a larger vision—one that leads to stability, flexibility, and ultimately independence.

An exit strategy is not about leaving real estate or abandoning your portfolio. Instead, it is about having a clear plan for how your assets will serve you over time. This includes how you will manage debt, generate income, reduce risk, and eventually transition from active growth to sustained financial freedom. Bank statement loans play a critical role in this journey because they allow you to enter and expand within the market, even when traditional lending would limit your ability to do so.

The first key concept in long-term strategy is transitioning from growth to stability. In the early stages, the focus is on acquiring properties and leveraging income to build a portfolio. Over time, the strategy shifts toward optimizing that portfolio for consistent cash flow and reduced risk. This may involve refinancing high-interest loans into lower-rate products, paying down debt, or consolidating properties to simplify management.

Refinancing is one of the most powerful tools in an exit strategy. Borrowers who initially use bank statement loans may later qualify for traditional financing as their financial profile evolves. For example, after several years of stable income and improved credit, a borrower may refinance into a conventional loan with a lower interest rate. This reduces monthly payments and increases cash flow, accelerating the path to financial independence.

Another important strategy is equity harvesting. As properties appreciate in value, they create equity that can be accessed through refinancing or sales. This equity can be used to fund new investments, pay down existing debt, or create a financial cushion. However, it is important to use this strategy wisely, balancing growth with risk management to avoid overleveraging.

Debt management is a central component of long-term planning. While leverage is a powerful tool for growth, reducing debt over time is essential for achieving financial freedom. This may involve making additional principal payments, refinancing into shorter loan terms, or strategically selling properties to eliminate debt. The goal is to gradually shift from leveraged growth to debt-free ownership, where income is no longer tied to loan obligations.

Cash flow optimization is another critical element. As your portfolio grows, you should focus on maximizing net income from your properties. This may involve increasing rents, reducing expenses, improving property management, or repositioning assets to generate higher returns. Strong cash flow provides the foundation for financial independence, allowing you to cover living expenses without relying on active income.

Diversification also plays a key role in long-term strategy. Relying on a single property or income source can create risk, especially in changing market conditions. By diversifying across property types, locations, and income streams, you can create a more resilient portfolio that can withstand economic fluctuations.

Another advanced concept is lifestyle design. Financial freedom is not just about numbers—it is about how you choose to live your life. Bank statement loans provide the flexibility to build a portfolio that supports your desired lifestyle, whether that means reducing work hours, traveling, or pursuing other passions. By aligning your financial strategy with your personal goals, you can create a life that is both financially secure and personally fulfilling.

Timing your exit strategy is also important. There is no single "right" time to transition from growth to stability, but it should be based on your financial goals, market conditions, and personal circumstances. Some borrowers may choose to exit aggressively, selling properties and capturing gains, while others may prefer a gradual transition, holding assets for long-term income.

Another key strategy is legacy planning. For many borrowers, real estate is not just a personal investment—it is a way to create generational wealth. This may involve transferring properties to family members, establishing trusts, or creating a structured plan for passing on assets. Bank statement loans can play a role in building this legacy by enabling the initial acquisition and growth of the portfolio.

Risk reduction is essential as you move toward financial independence. This includes maintaining adequate reserves, managing debt levels, and ensuring that your portfolio can withstand market fluctuations. It also involves regularly reviewing your strategy and making adjustments as needed.

Another important concept is liquidity. While real estate is a valuable asset, it is not always easily converted into cash. Maintaining a balance between real estate investments and liquid assets ensures that you have the flexibility to respond to opportunities or challenges.

Long-term success also requires discipline and consistency. The strategies outlined in this chapter are not one-time actions—they are ongoing processes that require attention and adjustment over time. Borrowers who remain focused and disciplined are more likely to achieve their goals and sustain their success.

Ultimately, the goal of using bank statement loans is not just to acquire properties, but to create a system that generates income, builds equity, and supports financial independence. By understanding and implementing long-term exit strategies, you can transform your portfolio into a powerful engine for wealth and freedom.

As this series comes to a close, remember that the knowledge you have gained is a foundation. The real value comes from applying these principles in your own life, making strategic decisions, and staying committed to your long-term vision.

Real-Life Math Example: Building and Transitioning to Financial Freedom

To illustrate how long-term exit strategies work in practice, let's walk through a detailed example involving a borrower named Daniel, who uses bank statement loans to build and eventually stabilize a real estate portfolio.

Daniel starts with a business generating $30,000 per month in deposits. Using a 50% expense factor, his qualifying income is $15,000 per month. He purchases his first property for $400,000 with a 20% down payment, resulting in a loan amount of $320,000. His monthly payment is $2,500, and the property generates $3,000 in rental income, creating $500 in cash flow.

Over the next three years, Daniel acquires four additional properties using bank statement loans. Each property generates an average of $500 in monthly cash flow, resulting in total cash flow of $2,500 per month. His portfolio is now worth approximately $2,000,000, with loan balances totaling $1,500,000.

As his business grows, Daniel's deposits increase to $50,000 per month, raising his qualifying income to $25,000 per month. He continues to leverage this income to acquire properties, but he also begins to focus on long-term strategy.

After five years, Daniel's properties have appreciated to a total value of $2,500,000, and his loan balances have been reduced to $1,300,000. This gives him $1,200,000 in equity. His monthly cash flow has increased to $3,500 due to rent increases and improved management.

Daniel decides to implement an exit strategy. He refinances two of his properties into lower-rate conventional loans, reducing his monthly payments by $1,000. This increases his cash flow to $4,500 per month.

Next, Daniel sells one property for $600,000, using the proceeds to pay off $300,000 in debt and invest the remaining funds into a diversified portfolio. This reduces his overall leverage and increases his liquidity.

Now Daniel owns four properties with total loan balances of $1,000,000 and property values of $2,000,000, giving him $1,000,000 in equity. His monthly cash flow is $4,000, and his reduced debt obligations provide greater financial stability.

Let's analyze the impact. Daniel's portfolio now generates $48,000 per year in cash flow, which can cover a significant portion of his living expenses. His reduced debt and increased liquidity lower his risk and provide flexibility. If Daniel continues to pay down his loans over the next ten years, he could eventually own his properties free and clear. At that point, his cash flow could increase to $6,000 to $8,000 per month, depending on rent growth and expenses.

Now consider an alternative scenario. If Daniel had continued to aggressively leverage without reducing debt, he might have achieved faster growth but with higher risk. By implementing a balanced exit strategy, he creates a more sustainable and secure financial position.

This example demonstrates how bank statement loans can be used not only to build wealth but also to transition into financial independence. By combining growth strategies with risk management and long-term planning, borrowers can create a portfolio that supports their goals and provides lasting stability.

As you apply these concepts, remember that financial freedom is a journey. Each step you take—whether acquiring a property, refinancing a loan, or reducing debt—brings you closer to your ultimate goal.

Chapter 15

Putting It All Together — From Approval to Financial Independence

At this stage in the Bank Statement Mortgage Loan Mastery Series, you have learned the full spectrum—from foundational concepts to advanced structuring, scaling strategies, and long-term exit planning. Chapter 15 is about integration. It is where everything comes together into a unified system that you can apply repeatedly to create approvals, acquire assets, build income, and ultimately achieve financial independence. This chapter is not about learning something new—it is about mastering how all the moving parts work together in real life.

The first principle of integration is understanding that approval is not the goal—control is. Many borrowers focus on getting approved for a single loan, but the true power of bank statement mortgage loans lies in the ability to control your financial trajectory. This means structuring your income, debt, and assets in a way that allows you to qualify not just once, but consistently over time. When you shift your mindset from "one deal" to "a system," everything changes.

The second principle is repeatability. Every strategy you have learned—from optimizing deposits to choosing between

12-month and 24-month programs—should be applied in a way that can be repeated. This is how wealth is built. A single property can create income, but a repeatable system can create a portfolio. The key is to document your process, refine it over time, and apply it consistently.

The third principle is alignment. Your loan strategy must align with your income, your goals, and your risk tolerance. For example, if your goal is aggressive growth, you may prioritize leverage and acquisition. If your goal is stability, you may focus on cash flow and debt reduction. Bank statement loans provide the flexibility to support both approaches, but it is up to you to align your strategy with your vision.

Another critical concept is financial positioning. This refers to how your financial profile is presented to lenders. Positioning includes your bank statements, credit score, reserves, and overall structure. Two borrowers with identical income can receive very different outcomes based on how they position themselves. This is why preparation is so important. By controlling how your financial information is presented, you can influence the outcome.

Income control is one of the most powerful tools you have. Unlike traditional employees, self-employed borrowers have the ability to influence how income flows through their accounts. By managing deposits, timing transfers, and maintaining consistency, you can create a financial profile that supports your goals. This does not mean manipulating your finances—it means structuring them intelligently within the rules.

Another key concept is leverage management. Leverage allows you to grow quickly, but it must be managed carefully. Too little leverage can slow growth, while too much can create risk. The goal is to find the right balance. This may involve using higher leverage during the growth phase and gradually reducing it as your portfolio stabilizes.

Cash flow remains the foundation of long-term success. While appreciation and equity are important, they are not always predictable. Cash flow provides stability and allows you to sustain your portfolio through different market conditions. Every property you acquire should be evaluated not just for its potential value, but for its ability to generate income.

Another important principle is adaptability. Markets change, interest rates fluctuate, and personal circumstances evolve. The strategies you use today may need to be adjusted in the future. Borrowers who remain flexible and responsive to these changes are more likely to succeed over the long term. The concept of financial stacking is also critical. This involves combining multiple strategies to create stronger outcomes. For example, you might combine bank statement income with DSCR analysis, refinance to access equity, and reinvest that capital into new properties. Each layer builds on the previous one, creating a compounding effect.

Another advanced concept is opportunity awareness. Successful borrowers are constantly looking for opportunities—whether it is a new property, a favorable refinance, or a shift in market conditions. Bank statement loans provide the flexibility to act on these opportunities, but you must be prepared to recognize and seize them.

Discipline is the thread that ties everything together. Without discipline, even the best strategies can fail. This includes maintaining clean bank statements, managing debt, building reserves, and staying focused on your goals. Discipline turns knowledge into results.

Another key concept is long-term vision. Financial independence is not achieved overnight. It is the result of consistent, strategic actions over time. By keeping your long-term vision in mind, you can make decisions that support your future rather than just your present.

The final principle is ownership of your process. You are not just a borrower—you are the architect of your financial future.

By understanding how bank statement loans work and how to use them strategically, you take control of your path. This level of ownership is what separates those who struggle from those who succeed.

As you complete this series, you now have a complete framework for using bank statement mortgage loans to achieve your goals. The next step is execution. Apply what you have learned, refine your approach, and continue building on your success.

Real-Life Math Example: Full System Integration from First Loan to Financial Independence

To demonstrate how everything comes together, let's walk through a comprehensive example involving a borrower named Sofia, who starts with a single bank statement loan and builds a path to financial independence.

Sofia is a self-employed consultant with monthly deposits of $25,000. Using a 50% expense factor, her qualifying income is $12,500 per month. With a 50% debt-to-income ratio, she can support total monthly obligations of $6,250.

Sofia purchases her first property for $400,000 with a 20% down payment, resulting in a loan amount of $320,000. Her monthly payment is $2,500, and the property generates $3,000 in rental income, creating $500 in cash flow.

After one year, Sofia's income increases to $30,000 per month, raising her qualifying income to $15,000. She uses a bank statement loan to purchase a second property for $450,000, also generating $500 in cash flow.

Now Sofia has two properties generating $1,000 per month in total cash flow. Her confidence grows, and she continues to apply the same system. Over the next three years, she acquires three more properties, each producing similar cash flow.

At this point, Sofia owns five properties generating $2,500 per month in cash flow. Her business income has grown to $40,000 per month, increasing her qualifying income to $20,000 per month. She now has greater borrowing capacity and begins to focus on optimization.

Sofia refinances two of her properties, reducing her interest rates and increasing her cash flow by $800 per month. She also improves her expense ratio by working with a CPA, increasing her qualifying income further.

After five years, Sofia's portfolio is worth $2,500,000, with loan balances totaling $1,800,000. She has $700,000 in equity and monthly cash flow of $3,300.

Now Sofia shifts her strategy toward financial independence. She sells one property for $600,000, using the proceeds to pay down $300,000 in debt. This reduces her loan balances and increases her cash flow.

With four remaining properties, Sofia now has loan balances of $1,200,000 and property values of $2,000,000, giving her $800,000 in equity. Her monthly cash flow is $3,500.

Over the next ten years, Sofia continues to pay down her loans. As her debt decreases, her cash flow increases. Eventually, she owns her properties free and clear, generating $6,000 to $8,000 per month in passive income.

Let's analyze the final outcome. Sofia has built a portfolio that provides consistent income, significant equity, and financial stability. She no longer relies on her active income to cover her living expenses, achieving financial independence.

Now consider the impact of strategy. If Sofia had not optimized her income, managed her debt, and reinvested her cash flow, her growth would have been slower and less efficient. By applying the full system, she accelerates her path to success.

This example illustrates the power of integration. Each step—income optimization, property acquisition, refinancing, and debt reduction—builds on the previous one. Together, they create a system that transforms a single loan into long-term financial independence. As you move forward, remember that this system is available to you. The knowledge you have gained is your blueprint. The results you achieve will depend on how you apply it.

Final Thoughts

As you reach the end of the Bank Statement Mortgage Loan Mastery Series, it is important to recognize that what you have gained is more than just knowledge about a specific loan product—you have developed a complete framework for thinking differently about income, lending, and financial opportunity. This series was never just about bank statement mortgage loans. It was about unlocking a new way of seeing what is possible when you understand how the financial system works and how to position yourself within it.

For many borrowers, the biggest obstacle has never been a lack of income. It has been a lack of alignment between how they earn money and how lenders evaluate that income. Traditional systems were built around predictable, salaried employment, but the modern economy is far more dynamic. Entrepreneurs, self-employed professionals, freelancers, and investors generate income in ways that do not always fit neatly into conventional guidelines. Bank statement mortgage loans exist to bridge that gap, but more importantly, they represent a shift toward recognizing real financial strength rather than just what is shown on a tax return.

Throughout this series, you have learned that qualification is not just about numbers—it is about strategy. You have seen how the same income can produce different outcomes depending on how it is structured, documented, and presented. You have learned how to choose between programs, optimize expense ratios, manage deposits, and position your financial profile for success. These are not just technical skills; they are strategic advantages that can change the trajectory of your financial life.

One of the most powerful lessons in this journey is that control is within your reach. Unlike traditional employees who have limited influence over how their income is perceived, self-employed borrowers have the ability to shape their financial narrative. By managing how income flows through your accounts, maintaining consistency, and preparing your documentation, you can influence how lenders evaluate your profile. This level of control is a significant advantage when used correctly.

Another key takeaway is the importance of preparation. Success in bank statement lending does not happen by chance. It is the result of deliberate actions taken over time. Clean bank statements, consistent deposits, strong reserves, and thoughtful structuring are all part of a larger process. Borrowers who prepare in advance are able to move quickly when opportunities arise, while those who do not are often left reacting to circumstances rather than controlling them. You have also seen how these loans can be used not just for approval, but for growth. Bank statement mortgage loans can serve as the foundation for building a real estate portfolio, generating cash flow, and creating long-term wealth. When combined with strategies such as refinancing, equity extraction, and reinvestment, they become a powerful engine for financial expansion. This is where the true potential lies—not in a single transaction, but in the ability to repeat and scale your success.

At the same time, this journey has highlighted the importance of balance. Growth is important, but so is stability. Leverage can accelerate progress, but it must be managed carefully. Cash flow must be prioritized, reserves must be maintained, and risk must be understood. Financial success is not just about how quickly you can grow—it is about how sustainably you can maintain that growth over time.

Another critical lesson is adaptability. The financial landscape is constantly changing. Interest rates rise and fall, markets shift, and personal circumstances evolve. The strategies that work today may need to be adjusted tomorrow. By understanding the principles behind bank statement lending, you are equipped to adapt to these changes and continue moving forward, regardless of external conditions.

Perhaps the most important realization is that financial independence is not a single event—it is a process. It is built through consistent, strategic actions over time. Each decision you make, each property you acquire, each loan you structure contributes to a larger picture. The path may not always be linear, but with the right knowledge and discipline, it is always moving forward.

You should also understand that setbacks are part of the process. Not every deal will go as planned, not every application will be perfect, and not every strategy will produce immediate results. What matters is your ability to learn, adjust, and continue. The knowledge you have gained in this series gives you the tools to navigate challenges and turn them into opportunities.

Another important aspect of this journey is mindset. The way you think about money, debt, and opportunity will shape your outcomes. Bank statement loans challenge the traditional mindset by showing that income is not just what is reported—it is what is real. When you begin to see your financial situation through this lens, you start to recognize opportunities that others may overlook.

It is also important to surround yourself with the right people. Building a strong team of mortgage professionals, real estate experts, and financial advisors can make a significant difference in your success. These individuals can help you identify opportunities, structure deals, and avoid common pitfalls. Success is rarely achieved alone—it is built through collaboration and expertise.

As you move forward, remember that the strategies in this series are tools. How you use them will determine your results. Some borrowers may use bank statement loans to purchase a single home and improve their quality of life. Others may use them to build a portfolio, generate income, and achieve financial independence. There is no single path—only the one that aligns with your goals.

Take a moment to reflect on where you are now compared to where you started. You have gained a comprehensive understanding of a complex and powerful area of lending. You have learned how to analyze, structure, and execute strategies that can open doors and create opportunities. Most importantly, you have developed the confidence to take action.

The next step is yours.

Whether you are preparing for your first loan, planning your next investment, or refining your long-term strategy, the principles in this series will guide you. Apply them consistently, remain disciplined, and continue learning.

Financial success is not reserved for a select few—it is available to those who understand the system and are willing to act. As you close this chapter, remember that this is not the end of your journey—it is the beginning of a new phase. You now have the knowledge to move forward with clarity and purpose. The opportunities are there. The strategies are in your hands. The only question that remains is how you will use them.

Your financial future is not determined by limitations—it is defined by the decisions you make starting today.

How to Get a Personalized Bank Statement Mortgage Review

If you found this book helpful, you may want to see how these strategies apply to your specific financial situation.

Bank statement mortgage lending is highly customized—your deposits, income patterns, expense ratios, credit profile, property type, and long-term goals all play a role in determining what you qualify for and how your loan should be structured.

Every borrower's situation is different. The way your income flows through your accounts, how your business operates, your credit history, the property you are purchasing or refinancing, and current lender guidelines all impact your options. The strategies and examples in this book are designed to teach you how bank statement mortgage loans work—but your actual qualifying income, loan amount, and loan structure can only be determined by analyzing your real financial profile.

If you would like a no-obligation Bank Statement Mortgage review, you can request one here:

Email: info@FinibiMortgage.com

A licensed mortgage broker will review your bank statements, income structure, credit profile, and goals, and explain what bank statement mortgage options may be available to you—including:

• 12-month and 24-month bank statement programs• Personal vs business bank statement qualification• Primary residence and investment property financing• Cash-out refinance and equity access strategies• Advanced structuring to maximize qualifying income

No cost. No pressure. No obligation.

Sincerely,

Joseph G. Correa

Finibi Mortgage Inc.Licensed Mortgage Broker

About the Author

Joseph G. Correa is a licensed mortgage broker and the founder of Finibi Mortgage, a Florida-based brokerage specializing in bank statement mortgage loans, non-QM lending, and strategic real estate financing solutions for self-employed borrowers, entrepreneurs, and investors.

With more than two decades of experience in mortgage lending, underwriting, and deal structuring, Joseph has helped thousands of clients qualify for real estate using alternative income documentation, unlocking opportunities that traditional lending often restricts.

Unlike traditional loan officers who rely strictly on tax returns and W-2 income, Joseph's approach focuses on real cash flow, income structuring, and financial strategy. He believes that borrowers should not be limited by how income is reported on paper, but instead empowered by how income is actually earned and managed.

Joseph is widely recognized for his expertise in:

• Bank statement mortgage loans• Self-employed borrower financing• Non-QM and alternative income lending• Investment property and portfolio financing• Cash-out refinance and equity strategies• Advanced mortgage loan structuring

Through his education platform, Finibi Academy, Joseph has trained tens of thousands of students worldwide in mortgage strategy, real estate investing, credit optimization, and financial independence.

He created the **Bank Statement Mortgage Loan Mastery Series** to provide a clear, step-by-step roadmap for borrowers and professionals who want to qualify for real estate without relying on traditional income documentation.

His mission is simple: To help people use their real income—not just their tax returns—to qualify, invest, and build long-term wealth.

When he is not structuring loans or writing, Joseph works with clients across the United States to design customized mortgage strategies that align with their financial goals, income structure, and long-term investment plans.

The Bank Statement Mortgage Loan Mastery Series Roadmap: The Complete Guide to Qualifying for Real Estate Using Bank Statements Instead of Tax Returns

The purpose of the **Bank Statement Mortgage Loan Mastery Series** is to give borrowers, investors, and mortgage professionals the exact strategies used by lenders and underwriters—translated into simple, practical steps you can apply in real life.

This series takes you from beginner to advanced mastery of how to qualify, structure, and scale real estate financing using bank statements instead of traditional income.

Each book builds on the last. You are not just learning how to get approved—you are learning how to control your approvals.

Book 1 — Bank Statement Mortgage Loan Mastery

Learn how bank statement loans work, how income is calculated, and why tax returns are no longer required for many borrowers.

Book 2 — Personal Bank Statement Mortgage Loans

Learn how to qualify using personal accounts, structure deposits, and maximize usable income.

Book 3 — Business Bank Statement Mortgage Loans

Understand how lenders analyze business revenue, apply expense ratios, and use P&Ls.

Book 4 — Bank Statement Loans for Self-Employed Borrowers

Master how entrepreneurs qualify and structure income for approval.

Book 5 — Bank Statement Loans for Primary Residences

Learn how to buy or refinance your home using bank statement income.

Book 6 — Bank Statement Loans for Investment Properties

Discover how to scale rental portfolios using bank statement + DSCR strategies.

Book 7 — Jumbo Bank Statement Mortgage Loans

Learn how to finance high-value properties with advanced requirements and structuring.

Book 8 — Bank Statement Loan Refinancing & Cash-Out Strategies

Unlock equity, reduce payments, and reinvest capital using bank statement refinancing.

Book 9 — Bank Statement Loans with Credit Challenges

Learn how to qualify even with lower credit using compensating factors and strategy.

Book 10 — Advanced Bank Statement Mortgage Loan Structuring

Engineer approvals using deposits, expense ratios, and lender guidelines.

This series is designed to move you from understanding → execution → mastery.

By the end, you will not just know how to qualify—you will know how to structure deals like a professional.

Educational & Financial Disclaimer

The **Bank Statement Mortgage Loan Mastery Series** is intended for educational and informational purposes only.

This content is designed to help readers understand bank statement mortgage lending, real estate financing strategies, and income structuring concepts. It is not financial, legal, tax, or investment advice.

Joseph G. Correa and Live Stronger Faster are not acting as your personal financial advisor, attorney, accountant, or mortgage professional through this publication.

Mortgage guidelines, underwriting standards, interest rates, and loan programs vary by lender and may change at any time without notice.

All examples in this series are for illustration purposes only and do not guarantee approval or results.

Always consult with licensed professionals before making financial decisions.

Risk Disclosure

Bank statement mortgage lending and real estate investing involve risk.

Income fluctuations, interest rate changes, market conditions, and lender guidelines can all impact loan approval and financial outcomes.

Borrowing against real estate or using leverage increases both potential returns and risks.

Failure to repay a loan may result in foreclosure and loss of property.

Cash flow, rental income, and appreciation are not guaranteed.

All strategies in this series are educational and must be evaluated based on your individual financial situation.

You are solely responsible for your financial decisions.